D1603190

Deanna Durbin

A Hollywood Fairy Tale:
The Legend of Edna Mae

By William Harper

Deanna Durbin: A Hollywood Fairy Tale: The Legend of Edna Mae
By William Harper
Copyright © 2020 William Harper
No part of this book may be reproduced in any form or by any means, electronic, mechanical, digital, photocopying, or recording, except for inclusion of a review, without permission in writing from the publisher or Author.
All photographs used are either from the collection of Stephen Cox or the author. In publishing these photographs there was no copyright infringement intended. Most of them were publicity promotions from Universal Studios.

Published in the USA by:

BearManor Media
4700 Millenia Blvd.
Suite 175 PMB 90497
Orlando, FL 32839
www.bearmanormedia.com

Paperback ISBN 978-1-62933-571-1
Case ISBN 978-1-62933-572-8
BearManor Media, Albany, Georgia
Printed in the United States of America
Book design by Robbie Adkins, www.adkinsconsult.com

Dedication
To the memory of
Deanna Durbin David
and for her children
Jessica and Peter
and the legion of faithful fans through the years.

DEANNA DURBIN

TABLE OF CONTENTS

Acknowledgements vi
Introduction vii
Motion Pictures 1
Edna Mae Durbin 5
Three Smart Girls. 9
One Hundred Men and a Girl. 13
Mad About Music 18
That Certain Age 21
Three Smart Girls Grow Up 24
First Love. 26
It's a Date 29
Spring Parade. 31
Nice Girl?. 33
It Started with Eve. 36
War Year Activities. 39
The Amazing Mrs. Holliday 42
Hers to Hold 45
His Butler's Sister. 48
Christmas Holiday. 51
Photo Gallery. 58
Can't Help Singing. 74
Lady on a Train 77
Because of Him 80
I'll Be Yours 82
Something in the Wind. 84
Up in Central Park. 87
For the Love of Mary. 89
Afterwards 93
Afterwords – medleys 99

ACKNOWLEDGEMENTS

There is always someone to thank, but for me the greatest thanks belongs to God and any praise to His glory.

A special thanks to my two youngest children, Rosalynda and Kolbe, who watched many of the Deanna Durbin videos with me. To Rosalynda and my oldest daughter, Victoria Bleu, a "thanks" for pouring over this manuscript, making suggestions and spell checking, and Robbie Adkins for book design and fantastic cover. To Stone Wallace for editing suggestions. No weight of responsibility is on their shoulders for the spirit and ambience of the material within. A posthumous thanks to Deanna Durbin who received my numerous letters for years – never answering but allowing me to share my thoughts concerning her acting abilities and singing. She did select a photograph from her collection and surprised me with her "smile" and autograph.

I need to mention those persons who attended the various Deanna Durbin Festival of movies I initiated at various locations in my area. To see smiles, hear laughter and remembrances and first-time viewer amazement, made the time and effort worthwhile.

I know my beloved wife, Teresa, would have enjoyed Deanna if she had ever seen her, but as a family we watched no commercial television programming and a limited number of videos. After her death in 1997 I found myself with more time for videos and there I met Deanna Durbin.

Finally, I thank you, the reader, for reading these words and hope you will get as much pleasure from them as I did in writing them!

INTRODUCTION
(Begun September 2007, revised Jan 2019)

I imagine in many male psyches there develop fantasies about certain movie actresses contingent on a silver screen portrayal in the darkened theaters of their youth. Even if I am wrong about others, I experienced this with my first silver screen "crush" in 1952 when I saw Jane Wyman in *The Story of Will Rogers*. Later this faux intimacy deepened when I viewed a full-page photograph in a movie magazine of Wyman in a dance pose with a light blue gauze- like dress that excited my naive adolescent id (viewing the photograph, at a later age, I realized its provocative nature). However, by the time she had her own TV show, *Jane Wyman Presents the Fireside Theater* (1955) I was no longer infatuated!

This feeling would not emerge again until 1965 on viewing *The Sound of Music*. This time the object of my amour was lively Julie Andrews. She was the talk of the movie world; her photograph on covers of all the major magazines. However, this was a short-lived flirtation as her next movie, *Torn Curtain* (1966), nixed the wide-eyed innocence that attracted me!

As I look over these words I just typed I am cognizant my ideal "silver screen" girl was a beauty whose movie roles conveyed innocence.

During the late 30s to mid-40s another girl sang and acted her way into America's heart, but I wouldn't discover her for many years. When I did, I almost immediately crowned her my newest silver screen sweetheart. While watching a video from Universal Studios Archives in 2003 there she was, inviting viewers to purchase and experience what made her the highest paid and most popular star of her era, and then "poof" she was gone.

The name "Deanna Durbin" did not conjure up memories, but I was intrigued! I ordered the Deanna Durbin Sweetheart Pack (a two-disc six movie DVD). After viewing all six selections I was totally captivated – here was beauty and innocence! I soon discovered this aspiration of my idée fixe's last movie had been released in 1948. Her contract with Universal-International was not renewed in 1949 and at 28 she had given up Hollywood/acting/singing and moved to France, living in the environs of Paris since 1951, and now was 86 years of age! (I wrote these words in 2007). Deanna Durbin died April 17, 2013 at 91 years of age – "poof" she was gone forever!

I continued to collect her videos and searched for biographical information. The biographical information I found was conflicting and most of it copies or paganization of someone else's information. I did manage to locate all 21 of her movies on DVD or VHS (22 if you count the 1936 short *Every Sunday* with Judy Garland) over a three-year period. Included with one video order was an internet print-out of a short bio sketch which included an address for Mrs. Deanna Durbin David. I wrote a letter on the off-chance it was a current address. I was surprised with a personalized signed photograph from her!

This led to my decision to create a Deanna Durbin Scrapbook. Why a scrapbook? During the 20s - and through the 50s - scrapbooks were an extremely popular means of collecting information and pictures of your favorite celebrity. There were vast amounts of movie/radio magazines with pictures and articles as well as newspaper clippings to sate the appetite of an aficionado. However, most of the information was publicist-generated and not very reliable. So, I started gathering information about Deanna Durbin's life which, I hoped, would present insight into the life and times of an extraordinary film star as well as providing a springboard for a more academic study. Unfortunately, the number of photographs were unwieldy and locating and giving credit to the various photographers leaves my scrapbook with limited photographs, but nevertheless I hope it will please Deanna Durbin fans – and hopefully introduce her to new fans.

If you are looking for Hollywood sensationalism this book is not for you, but if you want a glimpse at the brightest and best Hollywood had to offer in the late 30s into the late 40s – read on!

Completed June 16, 2019
The Solemnity of the Most Holy Trinity
Father's Day

MOTION PICTURES

The first attempts at motion pictures date back to the Upper Paleolithic era, some 40,000 years ago when cave wall painters depicted animals with legs positioned in a creative fashion to give the appearance of movement. However, it was not until the early 19ᵗʰ century that the scientific concept of *persistence of vision* gave definition to the illusion of movement from a static depiction. Viewing a sequence of individual still pictures with slight variations of positions would give the illusion of motion due to the eye retaining the preceding visual image for a fraction of a second. This concept was first developed by French inventor Emile Reynaud, who patented an animation device in 1877, which was performed publicly in 1892, demonstrating projected images using reflectors and lens which gave viewers 15 minutes of "motion pictures."

In 1887, photographer Eadweard Muybridge arranged a series of twelve cameras on a California racetrack so the movement of a running horse would break a thread releasing the shutter at each camera site as the horse passed. The objective of this exercise was to settle a bet for railroad tycoon Leland Stanford, to prove that at times all four feet of a galloping horse were off the ground. This experiment set into motion a lecturing tour by Muybridge demonstrating his photographs on a moving image device. Muybridge's visit to Thomas Edison's laboratory in 1888 rejuvenated the famed inventor Edison's determination to invent a motion picture camera, something he had been toying with for years. In the late 1880s a host of similar motion picture cameras were also being "invented" in other parts of the world. In 1891 the Edison Company would introduce the Kinetoscope and in 1896 an improved model called the Vitascope projector, which is considered the first commercially successful movie projector in the United States.

CARL LAEMMLE

Into this dazzling era of motion picture history stepped Carl Laemmle, born in Germany on January 17, 1867. Carl immigrated to New York, but later moved to Chicago to join his brother. He began an eleven-year bookkeeping job with the Chicago-based Continental Clothing Company's branch in Oshkosh, Wisconsin where he would demonstrate a flare for promoting and advertising. He married Recha Stern, the store owner's niece and met Robert H. Cochrane, an employee of a Chicago advertising agency and a former journalist. Laemmle would also learn to speak English. This is when events in Laemmle's life moved into the realm of folk legend: He journeyed to the home office to persuade his employer to increase his salary which only resulted in finding himself without a job! On advice from Cochrane, Carl decided to stay in Chicago and use his savings to open his own chain of dry goods stores. One day, as he was scoping a possible real estate site his attention was drawn to a nickelodeon. He was impressed with the large number of people waiting in line to spend hard-earned money to experience "pictures that moved!" In short order Carl learned that with a modest investment he could realize a tidy profit. In 1906 he opened The White Front Theater and he engaged Cochrane as his advertising manager. Two months later he opened a second theater, The Family Theater, and in the same year he created Laemmle Film Service with Cochrane as his business associate. Meanwhile, Thomas Edison, after spending years in court fighting for the ownership of certain motion picture patents, finally got a favorable ruling. This decision led to the formation of Motion Picture Patents Company; a trust comprised of various companies determined to eliminate all other competitors. This rankled Laemmle, but when he balked, he found he no longer had any films to rent for his theaters. He then decided he would make his own films! Moving to New York in 1909 he rented a studio and created Independent Motion Picture Company (known in the business as IMP) and produced his first movie, a one-reel version of Longfellow's *Hiawatha*.

UNIVERSAL STUDIOS

After constant struggles with the "Trust", Laemmle was vindicated when on June 8, 1912, the U. S. Government filed a petition against the Trust forcing all companies generated by the Trust to be dissolved. It was a new day for Laemmle! He now had offices in New York, two on the west coast and a new company – Universal Film Manufacturing Company, simply referred to as Universal. In 1914, Carl acquired a 230-acre ranch in Los Angeles and a year later Universal City was opened to thousands of spectators taking daily tours of the facilities until the advent of sound movies.

"The only people who don't like Deanna Durbin, it seems to me, are people who've never seen her movies."

- *Remembering Deanna Durbin*
By Leonard Maltin
May 2, 2013 (IndieWire website)

EDNA MAE DURBIN

The world of the mid-1880s through the roaring 1920s was experiencing dynamic technological changes at a breathtaking rate. The invention of the incandescent light bulb, early development of television, photographic records, first successful air flight, gasoline automotive, telephones, first commercial radio broadcast, movies, etc. Edna Mae Durbin was introduced into this changing world on December 4, 1921 in Winnipeg, Manitoba (Canada) to Ada (nee Read b December 8, 1884 – d June 10, 1972) and James Durbin (b October 2, 1884 – d May 1, 1976), formerly of Lancashire, England. Edna was welcomed by her nine-year-old sister, Edith, who had been born in England in 1912. A year after Edan's birth the family made the long trek: 1,210 miles to the warmer climate of Los Angeles, California for James Durbin's health. Edna was blessed with good looks and the ability to sing songs with a clarity of tone advanced for her age. Recognizing Edna's precocious talent, her older sister, Edith, now a school teacher, took 10-year old Edna for formal singing lessons at the Ralph Thomas Academy. The story goes that Edith was so insistent she paid a share of the cost for Edna's voice lessons. From all indications Edna grew up a normal child, attending public school and doing what an average young girl did in that time period.

Edna was discovered in 1935 by Hollywood theatrical manager/agent, Robert Sherrill. Sherrill was aware Metro-Goldwyn-Mayer (M.G.M.) was looking for a child singer/actress to portray Madame Schumann-Heink, in her youth, in a forthcoming biographical movie tentatively titled *Gram*. Sherrill's attention had been called to Durbin's extraordinary singing and on hearing her informed M.G.M. of her talent. Since Durbin's formal vocal training had been directed toward operatic, she was a likely choice for the role. M.G.M. was impressed and gave her a short-term contract; however, Madame Schumann-Heink took ill (dying a year later) and the proposed film was cancelled. Durbin, however, was

already making a name for herself locally through public appear-
ances, singing over local radio and at the Los Angeles "Breakfast
Club" (not to be confused with radio's *Don McNeill's Breakfast
Club*), according to Blanche Lemon's article on Durbin in *Etude*
(February 1940 p76).

M.G.M. now found themselves with two young singing talents under contact, Edna Mae Durbin and Judy Garland. There
are several rumored stories as to why Durbin was dropped after
the filming of the 1936 M.G.M. 11-minute short, *Every Sunday*,
which starred both Garland and Durbin.

The most popular account is that after viewing *Every Sunday*
the M.G.M. front office misunderstood Louis B. Mayer's remark
"drop the fat one" or "drop the flat one," and dropped Durbin
when he had actually meant Garland.

Other sources claim the following scenario: Edna Mae
Durbin was contracted by M.G.M. studios and made a film test
but after Durbin's film project was nixed her contract expired and
Durbin was approached by Universal Studios. According to the
New York Times (Monday, December 21, 1936) Durbin had made
an impression on casting director Rufus Le Maire, formerly with
M.G.M., now with Universal who "persuaded the new company
(Universal) to hire her." At Universal she was considered for the
low-budgeted film titled *Three Smart Girls*. The July issue of *Hollywood Reporter* (clipping date unknown) magazine announced
the studio (Universal) had changed Edna's name to Deanna (mis-
spelling it "Deanne" in the article). At Universal she continued
under the tutelage of the vocal coach Andres de Segurola, with
piano lessons from Francis Minnerick, and acting guidance from
both director Henry Koster and the associate producer on *Three
Smart Girls*, Joe Pasternak. As they were preparing to begin production Durbin was introduced nationwide on the Eddie Cantor
radio show. In John Dunning's tome *On the Air: The Encyclopedia
of Old-Time Radio* (Oxford 1998 p224), it was noted that "a casting director at Universal introduced Cantor to a lovely 13-year-
old girl named Deanna Durbin." Cantor had been invited to the
Café Trocadero – an upscale nightspot in Hollywood – to hear
her. Cantor at the time was developing his new radio show, *Texaco*

Town. Fortune magazine (October 1939 p68) commented on the Cantor's audition: "... put her (Durbin) at $100 week on his new radio program along with Bobby Bream, singer/actor child star. The first week she got 4,000 letters. Cantor worked her into a permanent spot on his show." Cantor was one of the most popular radio stars in the country, reaching literally millions weekly.

Another story claims *Every Sunday* was shot after Durbin's name change and while she was under contract with Universal. It was speculated Durbin's contract had a 60-day waiver allowing M.G.M. to use Durbin if she was not making a film, but why M.G.M. would make this short at this time is not apparent. Interestingly, in the movie *Every Sunday* Garland is called "Judy." Durbin is called "Edna" though the credits list Judy Garland and Deanna Durbin. The movie is a Garland vehicle with most of the lines and animated singing belonging to her.

Lastly, there is a story that Pasternak viewed *Every Sunday* and wanted Garland for the *Three Smart Girls* movie, but learned she was under contact to M.G.M. and unavailable, so opted to use Durbin on learning that she already had a contract with Universal.

Fortune magazine (1939 often cited) offered the following: "Renamed Deanna by the studio (M.G.M.) publicity staff she went on payroll at $125 a week. Just before her contract expired, Jack Chertok, head of Metro's short-subject division, was ordered to make a reel with Deanna and Judy Garland. He rushed it through in three days, told the front office Deanna showed promise, and advised them to renew her for another six months. But nobody notified Sherrell. Deanna was let go."

Though, not answering the question as to why M.G.M. dropped Durbin over Garland, Joseph Pasternak did explain how Durbin was chosen for his and Koster's first American film. In his book *Easy the Hard Way* (G.P. Putnam's Sons, NY 1956 – as told to David Chandler) Pasternak dedicated an entire chapter to Durbin. His perspective is like the various versions above, but with a somewhat different twist.

Koster and Pasternak had developed the idea for a movie involving three girls tentatively titled *Three Smart Girls*. They envisioned the type of girl to star and had begun the search. Casting director Rufus Le Maire, formerly with M.G.M., suggested two possible youngsters who had screen tested with his former employers. Le Maire was sure they were planning to drop one of the girls. Pasternak and Koster viewed first a test of Garland, whose singing and acting abilities excited them both, only to learn she remained under contract to M.G.M. Next a singing test of Durbin was projected. Both men were mesmerized! They decidedly told Le Maire this was the girl they wanted and on learning M.G.M. had in fact released Durbin, she was signed to a long-term Universal contact. Having only seen a singing test Pasternak was surprised, on meeting Durbin and her mother, to find Durbin to be "shy, timid, scarcely willing, or able to utter a word." Because of this natural shyness Koster volunteered to coach Durbin on acting techniques. It was reported Durbin had a bad habit of biting her nails; however, the habit was used effectively in *Three Smart Girls*. In a close-up of her thinking and biting her nails she slips on gloves and tells her father she is wearing the gloves to stop her from biting her nails, which most likely was a technique suggested to her to help her to quit the habit.

It is reported Robert Sherrill, acting as Durbin's agent, took her to Universal Studios with one detour to Walt Disney Studios with the idea she could be the right voice for Disney's animated project, *Snow White*. She was ruled out because they thought her voice to mature.

THREE SMART GIRLS
(December 20, 1936)

In September of 1936 Deanna Durbin began her movie career in earnest as the shooting for the movie *Three Smart Girls* began. Durbin arrived at Universal during a critical time in the studio's history. During the early years the studio produced such notable films as *The Hunchback of Notre Dame* (1923), *The Phantom of the Opera* (1925) and *All Quiet on the Western Front* (1930), which won an Academy Award for Best Picture; however, in 1936 Universal was on the verge of becoming what would be considered a second-tier studio.

In those early years Universal created a European operation producing films for overseas viewers. It was through this connection that both Joe Pasternak and Henry Koster would be in Universal's employment when, in 1936, Carl Laemmle "retired" from the movie industry "selling" Universal to Standard Capital Company. Laemmle's departure was due to his son's lavish spending on the remake of *Show Boat*. Carl, Jr. was forced to obtain a loan to complete the project. In Universal's 26-year history money had never been borrowed to cover production expenses. The movie's cost ran over and Universal found itself in receivership and the Laemmles were unceremoniously removed on April 2, 1936.

The uncertainty of Europe during the rise of Nazism and the redirection of Universal under new leadership found both Pasternak and Koster in Hollywood. The "new" Universal Pictures, now under the helm of Charles R. Rogers, announced budgets would be cut. The studio would begin producing low-budget films, mostly melodramas, cheap westerns, horror films and serials aimed at a rural market. Universal, unlike many major studios, did not own or have vested interest in a movie theater chain.

Pasternak and Koster were initially budgeted $100,000, but as daily rushes were viewed the budget increments rose to a final $400,000, and the film went on to gross $1,600,000. *Fortune* magazine (1939 often cited) noted, "Deanna's name, originally ninth on the credit sheet, had moved up to first."

Three Smart Girls (1936) met with critical acclaim giving relief to Universal's financial woes. The *New York Times* (Monday, Dec. 21, 1936) review used a unique word to describe the movie: "musicomedy," and predicted it to be a hit: "Universal's most bally-hooed 1936 release is the daintiest, quaintest, most hygienic little musicomedy of the season, written, directed and performed with such evident sincerity that it may well be one of the box-office surprises of the year." The film, written by Adelia Comandini and adapted by Austin Parker, reveals, with the opening scenes, Universal's hope for Durbin's stardom hinged on her singing voice and vibrant youth. The opening scene is a close-up of Universal's "new discovery" teenage diva Durbin (Penny Craig) as she begins the opening vocal strains of *My Heart Is Singing*. The next scene is a panoramic view of a Switzerland lake (actually Lake Arrowhead, about 85 miles east of Los Angeles) with the beautiful music and vocals resounding across the lake and mountains as she and her two sisters, Joan (Nan Grey) and Kay (Barbara Read), sail on the lake. The actual plot of the movie begins when the girls hear news their mother, Dorothy Craig (Nella Walker), has just seen in the gossip section of the newspaper her husband and the children's father, Judson Craig (Charles Winninger), divorced for ten years and living in New York, was considering marriage to a socialite, Donna Lyons (Binnie Barnes). The movie story revolves around the three girls' trip to New York with their governess Martha (Lucile Watson), and the ruse used to halt the pending marriage and reunite their parents. The three girls' arrival creates havoc for their father as he has not told his fiancée, "Precious" Donna, he even had three teenage daughters. Donna's mother Mrs. Lyons (Alice Brady) assures her daughter if she acts as if she accepts the children all will be well. The girls devise a scheme suggested by Judson's business staff member Bill Evans (John King) to locate someone more Donna's age, willing to make romantic overtures to Donna with the idea it would change her mind. Bill knows the man to do it, Count Arisztid (Mischa Auer), a penniless heavy drinker, but a true Count, who agrees to do it for fare back home to Hungary. Bill is forced to leave on a business trip, but he sets the plan in motion to have the Count hold a magazine under his arm, appear at a night spot where Judson, Donna and others, except Penny, will be attending and flash it about. Through a series of mishaps, the Count drops the magazine on the floor. Lord Michael Stuart (Ray Milland) picks the magazine up, pays his bar bill, tucks the "prop" under his arm and starts to leave, Kay spies the book and thus draws Stuart into the lark. The comedy moves quickly but the plan backfires and Judson and Donna plan to get married immediately in Atlantic City. Mrs. Craig is due to arrive soon, causing Penny, so distraught, to run away. The return of Penny and the Lyons' women attitude calls off the wedding. The mother arrives and all is well! Through all this there is the under-current of budding romances between Kay and Bill and Joan and Michael. Two original songs sung by Durbin were launched in the movie, *My Heart Is Singing* and *Someone to Care for Me* (both with music by Bronislau Kaper and Walter Jurmann and lyrics by Gus Kahn) and *Il bacio* (translated "The Kiss") (Arditi and Luigi). A stellar supporting cast (look for Milburn Stone as the telegraph clerk) added to Koster's "style and attention to details" making for a delightful and charming movie. The film was nominated for three Oscars: Best Picture, Best Sound Recording and Best Original Story.

A trailer for the film reveals little about the contents of the movie, but certainly called attention to Universal's new favorite actress: "Watch Deanna Durbin Universal's Star Discovery." A scrolling quote by Eddie Cantor reads "Deanna Durbin possess more charm, more poise, more personalities than a half dozen of the biggest feminine stars in Hollywood today. To hear her is to adore her, to both see and hear her is to take her to your heart for all times." Heady words indeed! In the actors/actress credits, Deanna Durbin is listed last with the heading: "And Universal's New Discovery Deanna Durbin."

When the film was released Durbin was making personal appearances in New York. The *New York Times* reviewer reported that when she returns to Hollywood "she will live in a new house overlooking Universal lot . . ." with a brand new automobile from Charles Rogers, production head at Universal.

There is no evidence Mr. and Mrs. Durbin had any aspirations to fashion Edna Mae into a child movie star prodigy. Mr. Durbin, a tool maker (machinist or blacksmith – as listed in the Winnipeg city directory) with the Canadian Pacific Railway shop in Canada, worked as a machinist in California as well. Edith, who was a decade older than her sister, earned a master's degree from the University of California and taught dramatics at a local Los Angeles junior high school, and Mrs. Durbin was a homemaker. From all sources it appears Durbin's lifestyle was simple and quiet. Once she was brought into the limelight there was no drastic changes in the family routine. Signed to a contract by Universal at the age of 13 Durbin began earning $300 a week (using the Consumer Price Index for 2018 this approximates at $5,383 per week). This weekly salary plus an additional bonus for making a film certainly altered the families financial outlook. Universal determined to make the most of its investment and began to consume most of Durbin's day time hours. Besides all the training she received to cultivate her talent, learning her lines, voice training and scene positions for filming, she was also being academically tutored. Teachers assigned through the school board of Los Angeles worked with her three hours of every school day in the year until she graduated in 1940. The "new house" reported in the *Times* review was a three-room white stucco cottage where Deanna could relax and even cook between training sessions and/or filming. The press releases indicated she lived a normal teenage life; however, birthdays on-set, and constant concern and supervision to avoid scarred body limbs or recovery off-time does not make for a normal setting for an active young girl.

Elizabeth Wilson writing about Mr. and Mrs. Durbin in *Screenland* (1944) noted: "They are probably the least "Hollywood" of all movie star parents."

The nearly two-million-dollar profit return reportedly earned by *Three Smart Girls* literally lifted Universal from potential bankruptcy and set the stage for Durbin to star in a series of musical comedies.

ONE HUNDRED MEN AND A GIRL
(September 5, 1937)

Deanna Durbin's second film released the following year, *One Hundred Men and a Girl* (1937), again teamed Pasternak (associate producer) and Koster (director) and was even a bigger hit! Almost all the critics gave favorable reviews. Durbin was recognized for her acting as well as her singing abilities. *Variety* (January 1, 1937) reviewed the movie by declaring: "Deanna Durbin is a bright, luminous star in her second picture, *One Hundred Men and a Girl*. Its originality rests on a firm and strong foundation, craftsmanship which has captured popular values from Wagner, Tchaikovsky, Liszt, Mozart and Verdi." The film's opening of the Universal logo spinning with the finale from Tchaikovsky *Symphony No, 5* as background music, while the credits roll, Leopold Stokowski is shown conducting – pure cinema magic!

The movie's storyline revolves around little Patricia "Patsy" Caldwell's (Durbin) attempt to create an orchestra so her father, John Caldwell (Adolphe Menjou), and his unemployed musical friends can find work. At the film's opening, three of the major characters of the story are viewed: Mr. and Mrs. John R. Frost (Eugene Pallette and Alice Brady) as theatergoers – she somewhat enchanted by the music and he struggling to keep awake and appear interested in the performance. Caldwell is seen peering anxiously through the stage right exit doors. At the conclusion of the music, Caldwell attempts to get Stokowski to listen to his plight and is referred to the maestro's manager, Russell (Jameson Thomas). Caldwell, who becomes agitated at Russell's questions, is thrown out of the theater by the stage manager (J. Scott Smart). On the sidewalk Caldwell sees and picks up a dropped purse and attempts to find the owner. He tries to turn it in at the theater, but the stage manager recognizes him and slams the stage door in his face. Downhearted over the entire ordeal he returns home only to be accosted by the landlady's demand for overdue rent. He gives her money – the money from the purse and responds "yes" to her question of finding work with Stokowski. Patsy, overhearing the remark, flies into his arms, overjoyed. The next day turns into disappointment as she is not allowed to join her father at rehearsal because he claims it would make him nervous. But she decides to follow later, only to learn he has no job. Back home at supper time she acknowledges she knows he did not rehearse and asks about the money. He tells her and she decides to return the money to the address inside the purse. As it turns out it is the home of John Frost. Patsy returns the purse and when offered a reward she asks for $52.10, to cover the rent and bus fare. Somewhat amused by the answer and the whole event, Mrs. Frost invites her to join the party. The food spread is sumptuous and after a plate is prepared, Mrs. Frost learns Patsy's father is a musician who also taught her how to sing, which leads to Mrs. Frost asking her to sing. Patsy sings *A Heart That's Free* (written by Alfred Robyn/music by Thomas Riley) to an astonished but appreciative audience. Afterwards Patsy tells of her father being out of work as well as a goodly number of his musical friends. An offhanded remark from one of the quests; that what was needed were more orchestras – this remark and a vague promise of sponsorship from wealthy Mrs. Frost – sets Patsy off to do just that! Through a variety of comical situations, including practical jokesters Frost and his friend Bitters (Jed Prouty), along with other mishaps, Stokowski is drawn into the scheme, especially after being so impressed with Patsy's rendering of Mozart's *Alleluia* (from the motet *Exultate, jubilate*). One "joke" and a "false" newspaper article leads Frost to agree to put the "unemployed" musicians under contract for radio appearances. When the truth is revealed, and the whirl of events finally are straightened out – the deal is off! In a final attempt, Patsy and the musicians silently slip into Stokowski's home. When Patsy finds the maestro relaxing at his piano in his second-floor studio, Stokowski becomes flustered and demands to know her reason for being in his home! She replies, "I have 100 reasons. Do you want to hear them?" His "Yes" has Patsy leading him out onto the stair balcony as the musician stationed on the circular stairwell begin the opening strains of Liszt's *Hungarian Rhapsody No. 2 in C sharp minor*. When Stokowski's hands begin conducting, Patsy knows all is well! The closing scene has Patsy singing *The Drinking Song* from Verdi's *La traviata*. As Stokowski brings the music to its conclusion "The End" flashes on the screen.

Deanna Durbin's acting was applauded by critics; with her blossoming skills and a stellar supporting cast another blockbuster was made.

The critical acclaim earns the movie five Oscar nominations: Best Picture, Best Film Editing, Best Writing (original story), Best Music, Best Sound Recording and winning for Best Score. Universal revised Durbin's contract, increasing her weekly earnings as well as her bonuses for subsequent films.

Life magazine (September 6, 1937 p81-83) labeled the film as its "Movie of the Week" with numerous photographs and acknowledged: "At 14, though she looks and acts her age, she has fully-matured vocal cords. In addition, she has what most singing stars notably lack - a captivating screen personality." The years 1937-1945 were aptly titled "The Durbin Era" by author Clive Hirschhorn in his book *Universal Story* (revised edition 2000).

In 1938, famous 20th century classical composer Arnold Schoenberg was invited to present the Oscar for the Best Music (score) to music director Charles Previn. Although Schoenberg fell ill just before the ceremony, according to Alex Ross in his *The New Yorker* (February 18 and 25, 2002, *Whistling in the Dark* p183) article, Schoenberg "took pride in the fact his short speech in praise of the film was read aloud."

A *Fortune* magazine (October 1939 often cited) revealed, "her (Durbin) parents, as a legal precaution, petitioned the court to have themselves appointed her guardians and her studio given name had to be made legal to prevent its improper exploitation." The success of her first film convinced Universal to allot $725,000 for her second outing, the first having only a beginning budget of $100,000 which increased to $400,000 before completion. James Durbin no longer needed to continue as a machinist. According to the same *Fortune* article Sherrill suggested: "Tell them you're a real-estate broker – everyone else in Los Angeles is." Which he did! Later the designation changed to just plain "broker."

In 1938 James Durbin bought Sherrill's contract for $18,500 and took over managing his daughter's affairs until Deanna's marriage to Vaughn Paul in 1941. In *Fortune* magazine (1939 often cited) it is interesting to note that a telephone conversation concerning Durbin led both Rita Warner (Sherrill's secretary) and Olive White (voice student at Thomas Academy) to sue Sherrill for a share of his commission as manager of Durbin. White, who had called Sherrill's office inquiring about a job, talked with Rita, who knew Sherrill was looking for a child singer. Rita asked White if there were any promising possibilities at the Academy – learned of Durbin and recommended her to Sherrill. Warner and White collected $4,500 a piece!

In 1938 the California Child Actor's Bill, also known as the "Coogan Act" or "Coogan Bill" due to the mishandling of child actor Jackie Coogan's earnings, was enacted. The Law required parents or legal guardians to establish a "Coogan" Trust Account, thereby allowing the courts to assume a commercial guardianship to protect child actors and their earnings. In the Durbin case, according to the *Fortune* (often cited) article, the court "ruled that $15,000 annually be used for living expenses and education, that 5 percent of gross earnings should go to her agent (10 percent was the usual amount) and $4,200 a year paid her attorney."

Parents' Magazine (November 1940) reported: "– – Mr. Durbin was made her legal guardian, answerable to the court and obliged to put fifty percent of her earnings into a trust fund for her."

Durbin's movie success led to additional financial revenue when Mitchell J(oseph) Hamiburg, a Los Angeles representative of the Touraine Company, a New York-based sportswear clothing line, realized after viewing *Three Smart Girls* that Durbin's name would be a good investment for marketing children's apparel. He signed an agreement with Mr. Durbin, now manager of Durbin affairs, and licensed the Durbin trademark to different clothing manufacturers as well as for composition dolls, songbooks, writing tablets, cut-out paper dolls, etc. Hamiburg was listed as

Durbin's manager in several *Life* magazine articles (March 14, 1938/August 14, 1939).

Bernarr Macfadden interviewing Durbin for his *True Story* magazine (September 1938 p23) wrote, "She is indeed adorable – modest and somewhat shy in spite of her screen experience." He added, "And when she turns her smiling features toward you there is within the depths of her blue eyes personality plus." This remark is reflected forty-five years later in David Shipman's article in *Films and Filming* (via several web sites - December 1983): "And when you have been smiled at by Deanna Durbin you stay smiled at – –."

The financial success of Durbin's first two movies secured her future income permitting the Durbin family to move from their modest home into a much larger house in the exclusive suburb of Laughlin Park in the Los Feliz area of Los Angeles. The new home had a swimming pool allowing Durbin to participate in one of her favorite sports, swimming, without being mobbed by fans desiring her autograph, as was the case at public beaches or pools.

MAD ABOUT MUSIC
(February 27, 1938)

Bruce Manning, who assisted in scripting *One Hundred Men and a Girl*, joined Felix Jackson in writing Durbin's third film *Mad About Music* (1938). This film continued to enhance the career of Durbin by garnering excellent reviews as well as generating ticket sales. The film premiered at Grauman's Chinese Theater on February 7, 1938. As a special honor Durbin was invited to put her shoe and handprint in cement. She wrote in the wet cement: "To Sid (Grauman) – with All My Love, Deanna Durbin, Feb. 7th, 1938" and signed her full name. She was photographed embedding a coin in the wet cement, which has since been pried up and removed by vandals. As with all events at Grauman's Chinese Theater it was attended by a large and enthusiastic crowd. *Mad About Music* was nominated for four Academy Awards: Best Writing (original story), Best Art Direction, Best Music (scoring) and Best Cinematography.

This sentimental comedy revolves around a daring scheme and a mother and daughter bond. The film opens with Gwen Taylor (Gail Patrick) and her agent/manager Dusty Turner (William Frawley) celebrating the premiere of Taylor's newest movie, *Love on Trial*, at Grauman's Chinese Theatre where the founder of the theater, Sidney Grauman (playing himself), asks Taylor to leave her footprint in prepared sidewalk cement. Later Turner, excited at the prospect for Taylor's career, wants to tell her some good news, but it is "Tuesday" the day she receives letters from her daughter Gloria Harkinson (Durbin). Gloria has been sent to a private boarding school in Switzerland so her mother, Gwen, can pursue her career as a glamorous movie star unencumbered by a teenage daughter. The discussion includes the strange items Gloria wants, the current request being an elephant's tusk. Gloria ponders what her daughter must be like and even infers she would like to visit her. Turner reminds her that 10 years ago she was a widow with a daughter and now she is a glamorous film star. He soothes her anxiety by telling her that within a year she will be financially able not only to visit her daughter but tell the world about her. The scene shifts to Switzerland and Gloria singing *I Love to Whistle* while on a bicycle outing with the girls from the school. Gloria, to fit in at school, has created an imaginary father – a big game hunter – who sends gifts and letters describing exciting world traveling adventures. To give these stories credence she has the custodian Pierre (Christian Rub), a stamp collector, give her stamps from the various locations of her father's adventures. She is challenged by her nemesis, Felice (Helen Parrish), on the authenticity of the letters and photographs. Later, while being punished by writing on the board two hundred times "Young ladies must not make other young ladies eat photographs," Gloria asks fellow schoolmate Olga (Marcia Mae Jones) to finish the punishment because Gloria wants to meet a young boy, Tommy (Jackie Moran) at the confectionary. In a moment of rashness, to convince Olga to take over the punishment, Gloria tells a fanciful story about needing to go to the railroad station to meet her "father" who is arriving by train. Her falsehoods turn into a nightmare when the school headmistresses, sisters Annette Fusenot (Elisabeth Risdon) and Louise Fusenot (Nana Bryant), learn of the story and her "father's" arrival. In the carriage driven by Pierre she tells of her plan to give the flowers to some distinguished gentleman at the station and then go to meet Tommy. Her plan is foiled, however, when she is followed by some of the students, led by Felice. Resourcefully at the station Gloria engages a stranger, Richard Todd (Herbert Marshall), to be her "father – Mr. Harkinson." Todd, a composer, plans to spend five days resting. To keep Felice from spoiling her deception Gloria tells the desk clerk that "Mr. Harkinson" is traveling incognito as Todd and wishes not to be disturbed. When the Fusenot sisters visit the hotel to extend an invitation for a luncheon in Todd's honor, Tripps (Arthur Treacher), Todd's confidential secretary, meets them and learns Todd has a "daughter" at the school. Later humorous dialogue, in front of a mirror, Tripps argues with himself and "Todd," Todd interrupts and learns of the headmistress's invitation decides to accept and end the charade. On the walk up to the school Gloria meets him and explains her dilemma. The luncheon is a success for all as Todd regales the school administrators and fellow students with his many adventures. Later, at another school outing, Todd receives a telegram informing him that he is wanted in Paris and must leave Switzerland. As Gloria helps him pack she sees a newspaper with a photograph and article noting that her mother, Gwen Taylor, is in Paris. In a bold decision to see her mother, she stows away on the train. The story races through to a sentimental conclusion of mother meeting daughter at a gathering of the press where Taylor announces she has a 14-year-old daughter just as Todd and Gloria enter the room. Dusty tells Todd, "If there is any power of the press you have a family." The film ends with Gloria singing *A Serenade to the Stars* and Todd and Taylor holding hands.

The team of Pasternak and Koster were not responsible for this entry; however, Pasternak was the full producer with Norman Taurog directing. Once again, a first-rate cast of characters made for a satisfying and profitable movie.

THAT CERTAIN AGE
(October 7, 1938)

This lighthearted comedy featured Deanna Durbin in a more somber role compared to her previous movies. The opening scene is of a Boy Scouts rally where Scouter Kenneth 'Ken' Warren (Jackie Cooper) is being acknowledged for his pledge to send two scout troops to camp using donations raised from a musical stage production. He acknowledges Alice Fullerton (Durbin) for her part in the unfolding plans. She gives a rousing performance of an original tune written for the movie, *Be A Good Scout*. The scene shifts to the rehearsal of the charitable musical stage production.

Based on young love and the various misunderstandings accompanying it, producer Joe Pasternak, director Edwin Ludwig and writer Bruce Manning, ably assisted by Charles Brackett and Billy Wilder, produced Durbin's fourth movie, *That Certain Age* (1938). It is a simple plot: a young girl "Alice" played by Durbin is "smitten" by an older, world traveling, adventurous newspaper correspondent, Vincent Bullit (Melvyn Douglas). Ken and friends are upset when they learn Bullit's arrival for a relaxing visit at the Fullerton's spacious estate will be in the summer cottage where they are rehearsing. Their attempts to discourage the reporter from staying only serves to solidify Alice's infatuation with him, ultimately "falling in love." The second half of the film is focused on resolution as the relationship becomes evident to Alice's parents and the object of her affection, Vincent, himself. The attempts to make Alice see the folly of her actions seem to only increase her infatuation. However, in a surprising resolution, the matter is settled. Alice closes the movie singing another original song, *That Certain Age* (written by Jimmy McHugh/music by Harold Adamson). Giving wonderful performances were Irene Rich, Nancy Carroll, John Halliday, and Peggy Stewart (later to be a favorite western star), just to name a few. Durbin sings six songs, one, an Academy Award nominee, *My Own*, which was a big hit for her. The movie received one other Academy nomination: Best Sound Recording. The *New York Times* (October 10, 1938) review notes: "Deanna Durbin has a thoroughly matures soprano voice. Almost equally important, however, is her unique ability to make material which might be either saccharine or morbid seem not only wholesome but reasonably pleasant."

Durbin won the critics' vote for the best performance of the month by a cinema actress. In March of 1938 Deanna Durbin and Mickey Rooney each won a special "Juvenile Academy Award" – an actual miniature "Oscar" – for their "significant contribution in bringing to the screen the spirit and personification of youth, and as juvenile players setting a high standard and achievement." At the time the Academy generally did not recognize children performances competitive with adults. The last such award was in 1960, to Hayley Mills for her role in *Pollyanna*.

Fortune magazine (1939 often cited) reflecting on the success of Durbin notes, "Not since Pickford, or at least the early Temple, has the wholesome and virginal note in mass entertainment been so successfully struck. – – hers is a personality that children and parents, scarred and callow, can unite in admiring. – – Richard Watts, Jr. the sourpuss critic of the *New York Tribune* left a luncheon with Deanna 'determined for at least twenty-four hours to lead a better life.'" p66-67.

In *Life* magazine (October 3, 1938 p32,33) *That Certain Age* was the magazine's *Movie of the Month* and viewed it as Deanna Durbin's first romance. Following the spiel on the movie the article continued with a sidebar telling of a 23-year-old fingerprint expert in the Department of Justice being so impressed with a full-page portrait of Durbin in the March 14, 1938 *Life* (a pictorial spread of Durbin and Eddie Cantor in New York p23) that he formed a club. The formation and activities of the club were detailed out in the following pages. The Deanna Durbin Devotees, the name given the club, was formed by Nelson Blair, Paul Davis, Deryl Maddox and Jay Gordon. The fan club promptly surfaced fans throughout the US, Canada and a host of other countries growing to 300 clubs worldwide, which, according to the article "…if not the largest, surely the most devoted of fan clubs." Loraine McGrath of Lynbrook, L.I. was noted as having the largest scrapbook collection, 3 books, containing 1,500 Durbin poses, whereas A.T. Held of Columbus Ohio was the "champion seer," having viewed *Mad about Music* 144 times. The club published a mimeographed newsletter, *The Durbin Journal* (first issue dated July & August 1938), to be published monthly. "Sole requisites" for all Devotees were 50¢ dues yearly. Interestingly *Life* printed a short two-lined poem written by a fan about Durbin:

> "I'd like to be just for a little while,
> The dimple playing in her wond'rous smile …"

THREE SMART GIRLS GROW UP
(March 24, 1939)

Durbin's fifth outing, *Three Smart Girls Grow Up* (1939), was a sequel to her first film, *Three Smart Girls* (1936). Charles Winninger and Nella Walker, as Judson and Dorothy Craig, and Nan Grey as Joan Craig reprised their roles; however, Barbara Read who portrayed Kay Craig was replaced by Helen Parrish. The formidable team of writers Bruce Manning and Felix Jackson, who wrote *Mad About Music,* and the producer, director team Pasternak and Koster were responsible for yet another Durbin blockbuster. *Three Smart Girls Grow Up* finds Penny Craig (Durbin) attempting to play cupid for her sisters and creating only chaos. The opening finds the "three smart girls" arm in arm, dressed for Penny's birthday party, "rehearsing" correct etiquette for various party guests and engaging in lively banter. At the party Joan announces her sudden engagement to Richard Watkins (William Lundigan). During the night Penny is awakened by Kay's sobs and, quietly slipping up behind, learns from reading over her shoulder a page from Kay's diary page revealing her love for Richard. The next day a casual remark from Binns, the butler (Ernest Cossart), sets Penny off to find a boyfriend for Kay to take her mind off Richard. At the music school where Penny takes voice lessons, she invites fellow student Harry Logan (Robert Cummings) to supper. At home Penny's attempts to get her sister's attention with her remarks about Harry lead them to conclude he is Penny's "boyfriend." When Harry arrives, Penny does everything to get Harry and Kay close to each other; however, it is Harry and Joan who become attracted to each other. When it appears that her plan has failed there is a sense of childish embarrassments and Penny is sent to her room and the matchmaking attempts are momentarily quelled. Later at supper, the other members of the Craig family decide Penny can no longer take voice lessons in the hopes this will keep her away from

Harry without directly forbidding her to see him. When Binns brings supper to Penny in her room the conversation leads to the failed mission, causing Penny to think if Joan calls off her engagement, then Kay and Richard could be together. Much later Richard takes the sisters out for a diversion. Penny asks him to take them to Club 33, where Harry plays piano. Harry dances with Joan and tells her of his plans to move to Australia, where he has been offered a job. Meanwhile, Penny embarrasses Kay by telling Richard about her affection for him, and Kay slaps Penny. Penny is accused of being selfish. These failed attempts leave Penny only one last hope – for her parents to call off the wedding. During the preparation and decorating for the wedding, Penny's mother has no time to talk. Perplexed, but not deterred, Penny goes to talk with her father at his office. The scene at the office is touching as she and her father finally have their private conversation without business interruptions, thus clearing up everything so that "true love" can triumph.

The film garnered no Academy Award nominations, however, Durbin's rendition of an old wedding standard, *Because*, sung at the movie wedding, resulted in a best-selling recording.

Frank Nugent in his *New York Times* (March 18, 1939) review remarked, "(Durbin) is still her delightful self, a joyously half-grown miss with a fresh young voice, clear eyes, a coltish gait and the artless art of being as lovely, refreshing and Spring like as nature has made her."

Look for Charles Previn, musical director for many of Deanna Durbin films, conducting a rehearsal at the music schools with Harry playing flute and Penny singing.

FIRST LOVE
(November 10, 1939)

As Deanna Durbin moved from adolescence to debutante before the public's eye the writers were careful to craft scripts to make the transition natural and acceptable to moviegoers and her many fans. Bruce Manning, with an assist from Lionel Houser, wrote his fourth script for Durbin's sixth film, *First Love*. This "Cinderella" story featuring Durbin's first on-screen "kiss" was another box office success. The *New York Times* (November 20, 1939) pans the "kiss" with: "Could Songster Durbin hold her fans, who like to think of her as a wide-eyed child with a full-bosomed soprano, after that historic peck? For a thrilling ordeal Universal chose an ingratiating fairy tale about a singing orphan who loses her slipper, wins her prince." And the "peck" made front page headlines in newspapers across the country.

First Love tells the story of Constance "Connie" Harding (Durbin). Connie, a recent graduate from a finishing school, is spending the summer with her guardian uncle and his family. Before departing the school, Connie is pressed to sing a song. As she sings *Home, Sweet, Home,* she breaks into tears. Miss Wiggins (Kathleen Howard) shoos the other girls out and challenges Connie to face the world saying, "The trouble with you young people is you don't believe in anything. You're afraid, afraid of hope, afraid of happiness." With this admonishment echoing in her ears, Connie leaves for her mother's brother's home. She learns something of the family's dynamics: her uncle, tycoon James Clinton (Eugene Pallette), is always away when the family is home and home when the family is away. Barbara Clinton (Helen Parrish) is the mean cousin, while Barbara's mother Grace (Leatrice Joy) is an astrology fanatic, and brother Walter (Lewis Howard) is a bored young man; all are uninterested and indifferent with Connie's presence. The next day Barbara learns popular, handsome and eligible bachelor Ted Drake (Robert Stack) has extended a 2:30 horseback riding outing at the County Club. Connie is badgered by Barbara to contact Ted Drake at the club's horse stables and delay him from leaving with the others, especially female rivalry, Wilma van Everett (June Storey), until Barbara can arrive. Humor ensues as Connie works to stall Ted but falls smitten by his charm. When Connie learns of a ball at the Blake's home, she rushes about to get ready for the dance. The household staff chips in to see Connie is dressed appropriately even to the extent of buying her a dress and a beautiful pair of "slippers," but at the last-minute Connie is pressed into a household chore and unable to attend the dance. Of course, efforts to get her to the ball unfold and she leaves for the Drake's, escorted by six motorcycle police with sirens wailing. Just like Cinderella, she is reminded she must leave the Drakes by midnight. Through a turn of events Connie goes before the orchestra and sings *Spring in My Heart* (music by Johann Strauss adapted by Hans J. Salter with lyrics by Ralph Freed). Ted is drawn to her voice, not recognizing her as the girl from the country club. His father, Anthony Drake (Thurston Hall), recognizing his son's actions and smiles, is encouraged to think this might be the girl Ted will meet and settle down with instead of running off to the Amazon as Ted has threatened to do. Asked to dance, Connie dances with "prince charming" for hours and hours. Stopping for a breather they walk out on the balcony where Ted talks of leaving and being gone for six months which brings them face to face and Connie receives the "kiss," which was reportedly shot 12 times before director Koster was satisfied. Suddenly Connie remembers the time and flees, leaving a slipper on the stairs, just as her family arrives after being stalled by policeman Mike (Frank Jenks). Barbara, however, catches a glimpse of Connie leaving, and determines Connie is the "Cinderella" who danced the evening with Ted. In true "stepsister" fashion Barbara mocks Connie and leads her to believe a relationship between Ted and Connie could never happen. Dejected, Connie returns to the finishing school to earn a scholarship for the Teacher's Conservatory of Music, where most likely she will become, like many of the teachers, an old maid. Meanwhile Connie's uncle is enraged when he discovers Barbara has had the house staff "sacked" and Connie gone. He literally "cleans house," burning all his wife's astrology books and smashing charts, paddles his daughter with a brush, offscreen, and boots his lazy son through French doors. Meanwhile at the scholarship audition Connie has chosen the haunting beautiful song *Un bel di* (*One Fine Day*) from *Madama Butterfly* by Puccini. As she sings the last verse a "slipper" is brought into the hall and given to teacher Miss Wiggins. As the movie rolls to the ending, "The End" is substituted with, "And they live happily ever after." Using the framework of a classic "Cinderella" story Pasternak and Koster created another memorable Durbin film.

It is interesting to note when Mrs. Clinton asks Connie for her birthdate so she could create an astrological chart the answer given was Durbin's actual birth date of December 4. Look for Robert Paige in the ballroom scenes. He will co-star with Durbin in the 1944 film *Can't Help Singing*, Durbin's only full color movie.

First Love received three Academy Award nominations: Best Art Direction, Best Music Scoring and Best Cinematography (black and white).

As Durbin's movie persona was maturing before the eyes of her adoring public, she was experiencing real-life desires of the heart. At the premiere of *First Love*, she was escorted by Vaughn Paul, a cinematographer at Universal. Fan magazines were gossiping and columnists were having a field day predicting romance.

Prior to the release of Durbin's next movie in 1940, *It's a Date*, a news photograph credited to Roman Freulich was issued with the cutline pasted to the back which read: "In answer to foreign mail requests for souvenirs, Deanna Durbin cuts up gowns from her wardrobe in Universal's "It's a Date." The bits are sent to soldiers of England and France. The souvenirs will be carried to the front, according to the fan letters."

IT'S A DATE
(March 22, 1940)

It's a Date (1940) is another Pasternak production but this
time under the direction of William A. Seiter. A simple story of
misinformation sets off a love triangle between mother and sea-
soned stage actress Georgia Drake (Kay Francis) and her aspir-
ing stage actress daughter Pamela Drake (Durbin) and wealthy
middle-aged bachelor John Arlen (Walter Pidgeon). The movie
opens with Pam lip-syncing the words of her mother Georgia's
finale song *Gypsy Lullaby* (lyrics by Ralph Freed sung by Kay
Francis) at her final performance of the play of the same title.
Georgia is introduced by her producer, Sidney Simpson (Samuel
S. Hinds), to playwright Carl Ober (S.Z. Sakall). She expresses
her appreciation and excitement for the lead role in Carl's new
play, *Saint Anne*, adding she plans to spend her vacation time in
Honolulu resting and rehearsing her lines. Pam, who attends an
acting school in Maine, has come to see the play with an actor
friend, Freddie Miller (Lewis Howard), and to confirm Sidney's
visit to the school to offer his expertise. At the school Sidney
decides to have the students act out the second act of Carl's new
play as there are some questions to how the action should flow. As
Pam sings *The Bonnie Banks O' Loch Lomond*, ending the second
act, both Sidney and Carl become convinced this is a role for a
younger person. After the rehearsal Pam is called aside and told
she has the lead. Flustered Pam leaves the room. The two men
agree it best to find another play for Georgia and then inform
her of the change. To complicate the matter, excited young Pam
decides she will go to her mother for acting help. On Pam's ocean
voyage she meets John Arlen and becomes infatuated by his attention. Arriving in Honolulu, Pam is enthusiastic to tell her mother
of her good fortunate. As Georgia is busy, Pam begins verbally
setting a scene for Sara Frankenstein (Cecilia Loftus), her mother's companion. Georgia steps into the room reciting lines from
her rehearsal practice due to the "similarity" of the scene. Pam

learns her mother has been given the lead in Carl's new play and later, from a telephoned telegraph message intended for Georgia from Sidney, that he will call at 8:00 that evening. Pam arranges with John to take her and her mother to supper with the plan that close to the 8 o'clock hour she can slip out and take the call at the house in private. When John meets Georgia and their eyes connect, their mutual attraction intensifies the dilemma. Pam tells Sidney in no uncertain terms she wants her mother to play the role. Sidney tells her he and Carl will soon be there and explain everything. A whirlwind of activities and misunderstood remarks culminate at the Governor's Ball when Governor Allen (Eugene Pallette) announces John and "Pamela, – I mean Georgia," are to wed. The movie ends with the reverse of the opening as Georgia lip-syncs the end of the play, *Saint Anne* finale, Durbin's beautiful rendering of Franz Schubert's *Ave Maria*.

According to many reviews the *It's a Date* screenplay was thought of as "silly;" however, they applauded Durbin's maturing acting abilities and richer voice. The total effort of all involved made the faire enjoyable and successful. The movie introduced American movie audiences to S.Z. Sakall, soon to become a comedic fixture in many films of the 40s.

The movie was remade by M.G.M. ten years later titled *Nancy Goes to Rio* (1950), with Jane Powell reprising Durbin's role. *It's a Date* was re-released on video by Warner Archive, as M.G.M. had acquired the rights to the movie when it was remade.

Durbin appeared with Edgar Bergen and Charlie McCarthy over radio's *Chase and Sanborn Program* (April 7, 1940), and according to Old Time Radio historian Martin Grams, Jr., she was originally scheduled to star as the weekly singer for the 1940-41 season, but a week before the first production of the season, September 1940, her appearance was cancelled. *Parents' Magazine* (November 1940 p72) remarked, "Recently offered a radio contract at $7,500 a broadcast, Mr. Durbin merely opined that Deanna was already three weeks behind in her funny papers . . ."

SPRING PARADE
(September 27, 1940)

The successful writing team of Manning and Jackson, producer Pasternak and director Koster brought to the screen the romantic musical (music and lyrics by the team Robert Stolz and Gus Kahn) *Spring Parade* (1940), which, as a *New York Times* (October 14, 1940) reviewer aptly wrote: "installment eight in the endless success story of Deanna Durbin." The movie opens with a barefooted Ilonka Tolnay (Durbin) singing *It's Foolish but It's Fun* as she leads a goat to market in a musical tale set in pastoral Austria and romantic old Vienna. At market she meets a gypsy fortune teller who foretells her future which includes Vienna, meeting an important person and love. After an exhausting czardas dance with Gustav (Mischa Auer) she falls asleep in a hay wagon heading, unbeknownst to her, to Vienna driven by Latislav Teschek, the Baker (S.Z. Sakall). When she learns she is on the way to Vienna she balks and demands to be returned. However, she then remembers the Gypsy's fortune card and accepts Latislay's invitation to stay and work at the shop until his return to market the following week. She meets military drummer Harry Marten (Robert Cummings) who really wants to write waltzes and so Ilonka sets off to bring about Harry's dream. Of course, everything backfires comically, but the ending finds everyone happy. Bosley Crowther, in the *New York Times* (October 3, 1940), reviews Durbin's effort; ". . . she has never been in better voice, she has never possessed more charming grace and she has never — considering her advancement now to young ladyhood — been more pleasing to behold." *Spring Parade* was a remake of a 1934/35 release of a Pasternak European-produced film, *Frühjahrsparade* (literally translated from as "Spring Parade.")

Spring Parade garnered four Academy Awards nominations: Best Sound Recording, Best Music Score, Best Music Song – *Waltzing in the Clouds* (Gus Kahn, Robert Slotz) and Best Cinematography (black and white).

The movie included a cast of veterans: Henry Stephenson, Anne Gwynne, Peggy Moran, and Samuel S. Hinds, all giving performances that supported the lively story.

Bosley Crowther, reviewing *Spring Parade* in the *New York Times* (cited), remarked, "... it actually turns out to be one of the gayest and most delightful spots an excursionist might currently visit on the screen."

In 1940 a privately pressed soundtrack album of *Spring Parade* on six 12" 78rpm records was given as Christmas presents to those that were involved in the making of the movie. Only 25 sets were pressed, making this the "holy grail" of original soundtrack recordings (currently available on CD with additional material).

In the *Spring Parade* Souvenir Album issued by Robbins Music Corporation (New York 1940) the song *In a Spring Parade* (lyrics by Gus Kahn - music by Charles Previn) is listed and acknowledged to being "Sung by Deanna Durbin from the Universal Picture 'Spring Parade.'" In the movie Durbin does not sing a song by that title; however, in the "soundtrack album (mentioned above)" there is an instrumental credited to Salter-Previn titled *Previn March* (*In a Spring Parade*).

A remake of *Frühjahrsparade* (1934) by Ernst Marischka, the basis of *Spring Parade*, was remade in 1955 as *Die Deutschmeister* (*The German Champion*) with new songs by Robert Stolz. The movie was filmed in Austria in color.

According to *Current Biography* (1941), Mrs. Durbin expected her daughter to phone every morning and report her safe arrival at the studio. Durbin, at the time, was driving a gray LaSalle roadster, General Motor Corporation companion marque of Cadillac manufactured from 1927 until 1940.

On Durbin's birthday, December 4, 1940, she and her parents announced the spring wedding between Durbin and Universal cinematographer Vaughn Paul (son of Val Paul, a Universal studio manager).

NICE GIRL?
(February 21, 1941)

In the *New York Times* (March 27, 1941) the reviewers wrote *"Nice Girl?* Answers its own question by casting the relentlessly nice Deanna Durbin in the title role." In her first truly adult role, Durbin plays Jane Dana, the blossoming daughter of high school teacher and author Oliver Dane (Robert Benchley). The film's credits open on postman Hector Titus (Walter Brennan) delivering mail door to door in a provincial quiet town of white picket-fenced homes. This pastoral scene is contrasted later by Jane's remarks to her father, "I can see my tombstone: Here lies Jane Dana. Scientists and spinster. She died at the age of 82. A nice girl."

Jane, who is taken for granted by her childhood sweetheart, car enthusiast Donald Webb (Robert Stack), becomes infatuated with an older man Richard Calvert (Franchot Tone), who comes to visit her dad regarding a possible fellowship for his research. An impulsive indiscretion by Dane finds her alone in Calvert's New York home. Her return home the following morning in Donald's hot rod backfiring and blaring horn leads to Jane earning an unsavory but unjustified reputation by the townfolk. The situation gets more involved before everything is finally worked out after Jane goes to an army base, where Donald is located, after his angry departure and enlistment in the army. Jane locates him in the motor pool working on a transporter. He confesses his love with deeply felt words. The movie ends with the rousing *Thank You, America*. As the song ends the camera moves behind Jane to pan the crowd over her shoulder where the viewer can see "grease marks" revealing handprints on the back of Jane's coat resembling an embrace. An alternative ending was filmed for British audiences with Jane singing a somber *There Will Always be an England*, and without the "handprints."

The movie script was based on a 1930 stage play, *Nice Girl*, a comedy in three acts (without the punctuation) by Phyllis Duganne.

The film had originally been titled *Love at Last*, but released as *Nice Girl?* As the movie went into production Durbin became Aunt Deanna when her sister Mrs. Clarence (Edith) Heckman gave birth to a son, Richard (Dick or Dickie as he was often called) Heckman.

A suburb supporting cast: Walter Brennan, Helen Broderick, Anne Gwynne, Elisabeth Risdon, Marcia Mae Jones, and others added to the success of this feature.

An article in a fan magazine clipping (title and date unknown) titled "The Durbin Dilemma" discusses the notion producers "worry over kids who have grown up." A list of notable exceptions are cited for those who continued to act as youngsters beyond their age as well as a list for those who had grown up impossible to be passed off as children. "Deanna Durbin's ninth picture, *Nice Girl?* shrewdly prolongs her girlhood, but it is obvious she is not long for dolls and puppy love."

In an *Etude* magazine article Donald Martin (February 1941 p84) acknowledged "One of the most interesting musical personalities to have helped write the Hollywood history of sound films is Deanna Durbin – –"

The *Bakersfield Californian* (March 18, 1941 p11) "Around Hollywood" syndicated column by Paul Harrison reported: "Deanna is preparing for a picture called 'Ready for Romance.' The top man in it will be balding, hypnotic-voiced Charles Boyer." The *New York Times* (March 21, 1941), however, reported the movie with "Charles Boyer was abandoned."

1941 could be marked as the pinnacle of Durbin's movie career. She signed a new contact for $1,750 (consumer price index for 2018 – $29,965.71) weekly, a $50,000 bonus for each film and an annual increase of $250 weekly until 1943. Plus, annual income from "commercial interests" such as using her name on clothing and accessories, etc. put her up in the $200,000 (consumer price index for 2019 – $3,563,588.65) yearly bracket! In the same year Whitman Publishing Company (Racine Wisconsin) released two books: *Deanna Durbin and the Feather of Flame* and *Deanna Durbin: The Adventure of Blue Valley* for adolescent girls, written by Kathryn Heisenfelt and illustrated by Hedwig Jo Meixner.

Her private life became more public after filming *Nice Girl?* Durbin married Vaughn Paul on April 18, 1941 at Wilshire M (ethodist) E (piscopal) Church in Hollywood. The wedding was officiated by Dr. Willsie Martin and witnessed by 900 invited guests while a crowd of approximately 3,000 waited outside for a glimpse of the couple. Durbin was 19 years old. According to film gossip columnist Hedda Hopper, Durbin's mother was upset and wanted her daughter to wait, as did Pasternak. In his book, *Easy the Hard Way* (1956) Pasternak wrote he too was opposed to the marriage at the time, but was touched by the actual nuptials, where, according to him, Durbin invited Universal workers as well as front office management. Helen Parrish, who starred with Durbin on several occasions was one of the bridesmaids.

In another clipping, *Setting for a Star* (magazine title and date unknown), Durbin's home in Brentwood Heights, a neighborhood of other stars, is showcased. The house the couple shared took three years to complete. Durbin was involved in all aspects of the architecting and decorating of the single-floored "English type cottage" house. It was reported that the house was a wedding gift from the Van Paul's.

The rise to fame and fortune was bolstered by the discipline practiced by Deanna Durbin herself. She willingly gave up the normal life for the exacting regiment of a contract player. *Current Biography* (1941) outlined Durbin's daily itinerary of waking at 6:30 or 7:00 every morning, except Sunday, and working until 5:00pm. There were various lessons, but the primary work was the making of motion pictures. Durbin was involved with dual rehearsal and performances. Her songs were recorded separately and then synchronized with the motion of her mouth while filming.

IT STARTED WITH EVE
(September 26, 1941)

Deanna Durbin advanced from debutante to womanhood in the two 1941 releases: *Nice Girl?* and *It Started with Eve*. If *Nice Girl?* was "her first truly adult role" then *It Started with Eve* was a full display of womanhood in a performance of genuine talent against the backdrop of a sophisticated comedy. The movie was described by Clive Hirschhorn in his book *The Universal Story* (revised edition 2000) as a "unqualified delight." The film opens with a mockup of the front page of a newspaper with a screaming bold headline: "**JONATHAN REYNOLDS DEAD**" and editor Harry (Wade Boteler) crying, "Stop the presses, are you crazy? I got the best story since the Chicago Fire. The Herald's been getting all the good stories lately. What – you tell the advertisers that they can go to – – to the Herald!"

Jonathan Reynolds, Sr.'s (Charles Laughton) son Jonathan Reynolds, Jr. (Robert Cummings) arrives at the death bed with his father insisting he wants to meet his son's fiancé. At the hotel he cannot find his fiancé and her mother. Having earlier made eye contact with hat and coat-check girl, Anne Terry (Deanna Durbin), when outside they exchange looks and in a moment of rashness, he offers her $50.00 to "stand in" as his fiancé, Gloria Pennington (Margaret Tallichet). The next day, old man Reynolds awakes, declares he is hungry and wants to have breakfast with Gloria. This announcement sends young Jonathan whirling to locate "Gloria," who had told him she was returning home to Shelbyville, Ohio. At the station Jonathan locates Terry, gathers her bags and dashes off promising "I'll give you another fifty dollars!" Two of Terry's friends that went to see her off, stare at each other in disbelief. One of the friends, Jenny, (Sarah Padden) remarks, "Well, what do you know!" with Jackie Donovan (Dorothea Kent) Terry's roommates responding "Don't worry, Jenny, it's platonic. He wants her for his father."

The movie has an extremely sentimental moment as Jonathan, Sr. learns Terry is going home, made even more poignant as Terry breaks into tears singing *Goin' Home* (*New World Symphony* by Antonín Dvořák). Their "goodbye" supper at a nightspot and dance is a highlight of the film and referenced in the *Catholic News Service* Media Review Office's (1941) review when the reviewer wrote, "Laughton steals the picture in a sly performance that goes from deathbed to dance floor. . ."

The movie ends on a sarcastic quote from railway porter (Mantan Moreland): "Lady, the next time you ain't goin' no place, why don't you take a plane!"

It is Charles Laughton's role which attracted much of the reviewers' attention, but the combination of Laughton, Cummings and Durbin make for a great movie. The movie proved that Universal need not worry about Durbin's coming of age. The story is a delightful twist of misadventures and includes many of the elements of Durbin's prior movies such as "gold digging" daughters with determined mothers. In the *New York Times* review (October 3, 1941) Bosley Crowther describes Durbin as "refreshing and pretty as she has ever been − −" and goes on to write, "*It Started with Eve* is light and unpretentious fare. And the title doesn't mean a thing. But it skips to a cheery tune and should please—as they say—both young and old. It's the perfect "8-to-80" picture."

It was reported Deanna and Laughton had a fun time making the film and remained friends until his death in 1962.

The success of producer Pasternak, director Koster and actress Durbin continued. However, this would be the last time both men would work with Durbin. Both Pasternak and Koster left Universal Studios in 1941. The film earned one Academy Award nomination for the Best Music, Scoring of a Musical Picture. A stellar supporting cast included: Walter Catlett, Catherine Doucet, Margaret Tallichet, Guy Kibbee, and Gus Schilling just to name a few. Note: Look for Helen Parrish as one of the nightclub patrons.

Life magazine reported in its June 16, 1941 issue (p26): "Next to the U.S., Canada and Britain, Deanna Durbin is most popular in Italy. Last week Mussolini's own newspaper, *Il Popol*, burst forth with passionate appeal: 'Dearest Deanna, in the past we always had a soft place in our heart for you. However today we fear that you, like the remainder of American youth, are controlled by your President and perhaps to – will see fine American youth marching into battle in defense of Britain ...'" Continuing in this vain Mussolini calls for her not to "listen to yours and our enemies.'"

It Started with Eve was remade in 1964 as *I'd Rather Be Rich*, a Ross Hunter Production and Universal Pictures offering starring Sandra Dee and Robert Goulet, with a reversal of role as a young heiress is summoned to the bedside of her dying grandfather who wants to meet her fiancé.

WAR YEAR ACTIVITIES

The motion picture industry supported the war effort by increasing film production, releasing an average of a feature a week, so to satisfy and placate a troubled nation's continual need for escapist entertainment. The box office had never been so busy and according to wartime regulations the profits were to be used for improvements of facilities at studios. Many of the films were overt patriotic in nature and always depicted the positive. In *Hers to Hold* two shore patrol personnel order the lovers, Durbin and Joseph Cotten to leave the beach area, remarking as they watch the couple scramble under the barbed wire – one: "Nice lookin' girl" with the other responding, "See what I mean, Joe. It's things like that we are fightin' for." The topical nature of Durbin working in the aircraft industry gave the viewer a glimpse at the staggering build-up required to meet the demands for airplane production for the war effort as well as the heartbreak couples experienced due to separation by enlistment or out of country deployments.

In *The Great Movie Stars: The Golden Age* (Hill and Wang revised edition 1970 p182-184), David Shipman wrote: "In 1942 there was a unique programme playing the Odeon circuit throughout Britain: The Deanna Durbin Festival." Seven days of Durbin films played to packed cinemas. He continues, "Durbin's popularity was considerably greater in Britain than the US: in Britain during the four years 1939-42 she was easily the top female box office draw – –"

Newly married Deanna Durbin returned to work and in 1942, Paul enlisted in the Navy. As a supportive wife Durbin began to direct her time and support on behalf of the servicemen by touring bases, visiting "canteens" and USOs to boost moral with her visits and singing. The USO which was incorporated in 1941 with centers and clubs around the world gave GI's a "home away from home" and the Hollywood Canteen, founded by Bette Davis and John Garfield, which opened its doors on October 3,

1942, was modeled after the Stage Door Canteen in New York which opened March 2, 1942, where servicemen could go to listen to music, eat, dance, and rub "shoulders" with "stars" in a nonalcoholic environment. As the canteens spread throughout the country Durbin would tour, signing autographs, chatting and dancing with servicemen. She was extremely supportive of the American Red Cross, which had begun a national blood donor program, before America's involvement in the war. The 1943 movie, *Hers to Hold*, opens with people flocking to the Red Cross blood donor station. As the camera follows there is a pause for moment, focused on the Red Cross poster stating: "Give Your Blood to Save A Life." It was reported Durbin actually gave blood in her opening scene. Even before America's involvement in the war Durbin had taken time off from the production of *Spring Parade* to make a newsreel appeal for donations to the war relief funds. A 1943 press release with a "pin-up" photograph of Durbin announced she, as well as many other stars "have long since forgone vacations and are fully devoted to motion pictures a war work." One of Consolidated Aircraft Corporation's manufactured B-24 Liberator in the 530 Bomb Squadron, under the command of Lt. Donal Engen, was named "Deanna Dreamboat" after the actress.

There were many short films with "guest appearances" by movie stars and singers produced to boost America's involvement in statewide activities to aid the war efforts overseas. *Shining Hour* (alternative title: *The Road to Victory*), a short film intended to drum up support for the Fifth War Loan Campaign, depicts a happy family in 1960 enjoying the prosperity and advantages made possible by the successful proficiency of the war, and how the sacrifices of 1944 have made the world a better place. Deanna Durbin is shown singing *Begin the Beguine* (written by Cole Porter) as performed in the movie *Hers to Hold*. The alternative *The Road to Victory* movie was an edited and truncated re-release of *The Shining Future* in the same year.

In July 1941 Universal announced Deanna Durbin's next film would be *They Live Alone*, based on an original screenplay by Sonya Levien and directed by William Seiter. In October 1941

Durbin went to New York to meet with Universal president Nate Blumberg to request more control of her films and permission to work for other studios. Durbin's insistence was rumored to be partly due to the fact she felt her husband was not being treated fairly as well as the departure of her mentor, Pasternack. Four days later Durbin was suspended by the studio for her refusal to make the movie and she appeared ready to continue the suspension indefinitely. *They Live Alone* and a second project for director Seiter, *Marriage of Inconvenience,* were canceled due to failure of finding an appropriate female lead. Durbin was reinstated in January 1942 after working out some details in her contract, especially the right for her to approve her directors and scripts. This was followed with the announcement that *They Live Alone* was again going to be put into production. A revised announcement in March 1942 listed *Three Smart Girls Join Up* as replacing *They Live Alone*. Later Universal announced all previously announced Durbin films had been replaced on the schedule by *The Divine Young Lady*, the initial working title of *The Amazing Mrs. Holliday*. Paul, meanwhile, had parted ways with Universal employment (information partly based on *America Film Institute Catalog 1941-1950* p63-64).

It was during this time frame that rumors of Durbin's disenchantment with Hollywood began to circulate.

THE AMAZING MRS. HOLLIDAY
(February 19, 1943)

The working titles for *The Amazing Mrs. Holliday* were *The Divine Young Lady*, *Call Me Yours* and, when French director Jean Renoir was assigned the film: *Forever Yours*. Some consider *The Amazing Mrs. Holliday* (1943) as Durbin's first dramatic role. Director Jean Renoir, son of famed Impressionist painter Pierre-Auguste Renoir, had his start in the silent film era. He directed both *La Grande Illusion* (1937) and *The Rules of the Game* (1939) which are often cited by critics as among the greatest films ever made. However, in the final credits of *The Amazing Mrs. Holliday* Bruce Manning was listed as director. William K. Everson's article "Deanna Durbin and Jean Renoir" (*Films in Review* magazine August/September 1986) tells of his writing Durbin to ask about the change? Durbin wrote back a detailed letter regarding the filming: "Universal contracted Jean Renoir to make a film with me because we all wanted to change, by then, stereotyped image of the 'nice' young girl, the sugarcoated 'Miss Fixit,' the kind of story Jean Renoir qualified as 'trop mini' (too cute). The French way of movie making differed from the American way. On the first day of shooting we only had a few pages of script." However, Renoir, in his autobiography, wrote there had been several weeks of shooting and, according to Everson, on a non-complicated or spectacular film, "imply that Renoir probably shot most of the picture." Durbin goes on to say: "... after a month of shooting we looked at a rough cut and Jean, Bruce and I realized we were riding toward disaster." According to Durbin, Manning suggested an adaptation of Shakespeare's *Taming of the Shrew* transposed to the present times in Texas and talked the front office into scrapping the present project. However, Renoir told Durbin, "he didn't think he could go on with the picture as he was suffering from an old war wound and was in great pain." Bruce Manning assumed directorial reign. After weeks of filming, Robert White was brought in to rewrite the ending. In September of 1942 Universal announced a suspension was required for further rewrite, and for the second unit of photography to film additional background material of the shipyards and also street scene background. The picture was resumed in October after significant rewriting on the screenplay by Manning and Frank Ryan.

Screenland (May 1944 p12) review read: "For the first time in her career, Deanna Durbin has to cope with a poor story – – hodge-podge script" with Durbin's character a refugee from the "war in China with a brood of adopted babies, then as a giddy masquerading matron, and finally as a lovelorn girl – ". The film can be viewed as drama to comedy as Renoir's artistic input ended, and Manning's more traditional American cinema took over. Even with the swift changes, the script's continuity accommodates the shift.

New York Times review (February 22, 1943 p20), simply signed T.S., slams the movie from the beginning of the review to its conclusion: "For 'The Amazing Mrs. Holliday' is essentially dishonest. Its laughs are manufactured; its tears are phony. It is a trivial story upon a theme much too sensitive and real to be exploited in such shoddy fashion."

The film as a drama, reveals the horrors of the war on children, explicitly portraying the odyssey of a band of waifs orphaned by the Japanese in China under the guidance of schoolteacher Ruth Kirke (Durbin). Once she and her array of children are settled in Commodore Thomas Holliday's (Harry Davenport) mansion touches of humor are introduced, particularly the antics of the Commodore's grandson and namesake Thomas Spencer Holliday (Edmond O'Brien) His falling in love with his "grandmother" brings the story to a surprising conclusion.

The movie opens at sea, where Ruth and her eight orphans, rescued from Commodore Holliday's torpedoed ship (Holliday and an orphan, Pepe, were assumed to have drowned), are preparing to dock at San Francisco. They learn the children cannot disembark without posting a $500 per child fee. Timothy Blake, the Commodore's steward (Barry Fitzgerald), at Ruth's insistence, goes to the Commodore's family for assistance. The family in the midst of settling the estate offers no help, forcing Timothy to blurt out that Ruth and Holliday were married. The problem of the children is resolved until young Thomas Holliday appears. He sees Ruth for the first time coming down the stairs in a lovely gown, coiffured and staggering, due to not being used to high heels. The press gets wind of the story and soon everything is blown out of proportion. Ruth decides to leave. She, Timothy and the children are caught slipping out in the early morning by Tom. After the children return to bed Ruth confesses to Tom she was not married to his grandfather. Through a series of flashbacks, she relives the horrors that led them to leave China to take the European orphans to Calcutta. Tom, moved by the story, agrees to adopt the children. It is agreed once the "marriage issue" settles and the immigration papers arrive, Ruth should leave. Timothy, aware of the feeling Ruth has for Tom, stops her from leaving with a humorous ruse that included actor Gus Schilling as her "fiancé," Jeff Adams, at the train station. The movie comes to its climax during a China Relief Ball, where Commodore Holliday and Pepe's sudden appearances throws everything topsy-turvy.

The trailer advertised: "Starring a ravishing new Deanna Durbin." Which certainly contrasted Renoir's demand for realism. Renoir insisted on scenes with no make-up in "China" (the hills back of Universal studios) while the scenes under the direction of Bruce Manning, shot at the Holliday mansion, portray Ruth in the dazzling gowns and sophisticated hairstyles.

A great supporting cast that included Arthur Treacher, Grant Mitchell, Elisabeth Risdon, Gus Schilling, Frieda Inescort, Richard Loo and others, added to the overall production.

HERS TO HOLD
(July 16, 1943)

Hers to Hold (1943) was the third sequence to the "Smart Girl" movies, with Penny Craig (Durbin) grown and without her two sisters. The opening has Penny giving blood for the Red Cross. Aviator and aircraft worker Bill Morley (Joseph Cotten) and his working pal Rosey Blake (Gus Schilling) have also just given blood. The men note all the scurrying around as Penny is escorted into a curtained-off area surrounded by an entourage of press photographers and reporters. Blake knows of her, daughter of millionaire Judson Craig (Charles Winninger reprising the role as father). To impress Rosey and get a look at Penny, Bill "masquerades" as a doctor and gets Penny's phone number. In a daring moment while holding her wrist on the pretense of taking her pulse, he kisses her. Suave bold Bill Morley is to spend the remainder of the movie daringly entering the world of the wealthy and attempting to win the attention of Penny. It is quickly evident Penny is in love. Rosey later drives Penny to the cafeteria where the aircraft workers take lunch; she dances with Bill and later, at a restricted beach area, Bill and Penny's conversation takes a romantic drift. When Bill is vague about their next meeting with a flippant remark about phoning Penny sometime, she decides to take matters into her own hands and joins Bill and Rosey at Vega Aircraft Corporation. The story, from this point, hinges on Morley, who is waiting for orders to return to the skies as a fighter pilot. Bill does not want to hurt Penny and goes out of his way to avoid her. His "heart" changes his mind and with only 48 hours left before he leaves, the two make the most of the time. A pivotal point in the movie occurs when Penny and Bill witness how devastated Hannah Gordon (Fay Helm), one of the working girls in Penny's section, is upon learning her aviator husband has been shot down. Penny goes to her father's office demanding and pleading that he use his influence to keep Morley from going to war. Judson gives Penny and the theatergoers a patriotic message of the necessities of everyone pulling their weight until the war's end. Bill, on the other hand, breaks off their relationship by leaving a note for Penny to read when she picks him up to take him to the party the Craig family is giving for his going away. The "goodbye" message states he will not be attending the party, and this sets Penny out to look for Bill. When she finds him, she confronts him, but to no avail and so she leaves, remarking in a blasé manner that "she understands." A disheartened Penny, though somewhat inspired by her father's words, returns home and mounts the steps to her room to dress for the party. At the opening strains of Penny singing the mournful *Pale Hands I Loved* (*Kashmiri Song*) (from a poem by Laurence Hope put to music by Amy Woodforde-Finden) the camera's focus moves slowly through tree foliage and spotlights Penny singing. Her father and mother climb silently and purposefully up the stairs, especially the father, as having moments ago heard her daughter tell him she would "die" if Bill should be lost in action. During the singing Penny reflects on the many happy moments she and Bill shared. The parents enter the room at the conclusion of the final verse:

"Pale hands, pink tipped, like Lotus buds that float
   On those cool waters where we used to dwell,
I would have rather felt you round my throat,
   Crushing out life, than waving me farewell!"

Penny falls to her knees and weeps into her mother's lap. Encouraged, by both her parents, she dries her eyes and continues her preparations.

Rosey, on learning Bill really cares for Penny, leaves a note for her at the party. The movie ending is one of mixed emotions as the couple must part for the "greater good" – her to build planes so Morley can fly them!

There is an interesting scene with the Craig family watching home movies of Penny growing up. Some of the shots are directly from the prior "Three Smart Girls" series as well as from other Deanna Durbin films.

This marked the first film that Felix Jackson produced for Durbin with direction by Frank Ryan and joined by an all-star cast that includes Samuel S. Hinds, Ludwig Stossel (Binns), Fay Helm and Nella Walker reprising her role, Dorothy Craig. There was an Academy Award nomination for Best Music, Song, *Say a Pray'r for the Boys Over There* (Herb Magidson, Jimmy McHugh).

A review from *New York Times* (signed L.B.F. July 22, 1943) reads: "Not, mind you, that the newcomer is any great shakes as a motion picture. At best, it is lightweight entertainment loaded with shopworn gags, situations and heart throbs. But in it Miss Durbin has a vehicle suited to her age and talents and the Durbin clubs are in for a grand time."

From an online offering of the *American Film Institute Catalog of Feature Films*, it was reported, "The working title of this film (*Hers to Hold*), was *Three Smart Girls Join Up*. According to a March 1942 *HR* (*Hollywood Reporter*) news item, Universal's London office purchased a story by that title from Derek Bolton, a flyer with the RAF. It was ". . . slated to begin production in May 1942, but it was shelved until Jan 1943, when Universal announced it had renamed the project *Hers to Hold*." Bolton is not credited on screen. This original title, *Three Girls Join Up*, was also acknowledged by *Silver Screen* magazine (1942).

HIS BUTLER'S SISTER
(November 26, 1943)

His Butler's Sister (1943) was tagged by reviewer Bosley Crowther in the *New York Times* (December 30, 1943) as Universal having a "tough time bringing Deanna Durbin to adult flower...in her two most recent pictures she plainly lacked her potential bloom." This film is centered around Ann Carter (Durbin) traveling by train to New York in hopes of a singing career. The musical comedy opens with the ditzy Sunshine Twins (Iris Adrian and Robin Raymond) dancing and singing *Is It True What They Say About Dixie?* in the aisle at the door of befuddled composer Charles Gerard's (Franchot Tone) roomette in hopes of getting a spot in his new shows. After the display, the frustrated Gerard tells the porter not to give his car number to anyone. The porter agrees; if asked he will give the number of an empty room. Meanwhile, before we even see Ann's face, we watch her making her way through the rail cars with every man, women and child acknowledging her presence. Ann, overhearing the Sunshine Twins talking about "the Charles Gerard," decides to audition for him. She asks the porter for Gerald's roomette number only to receive the decoy number from a grinning porter. Ann finds herself singing *In the Spirit of the Moment* to a lady lingerie salesman (Andrew Tombes), and receiving a girdle for her efforts.

Mr. Crowther in his review sums the story cleverly: "A little lady arrives in New York with the hope of putting her vocal talents to the service of smart young composer Charles Gerard. By a perfectly amazing coincidence her brother is this gentleman's butler, and the immediate service which the little lady puts her talent is that of a maid. Proximity provides occasions." The butler Martin Murphy (Pat O'Brien) sent his half-sister, Ann, a sizeable amount of money and his Park Avenue address leads her to believe he is wealthy. Crowther continues: "Misunderstandings create despairs. But eventually the social equalizer, sweet love, levels everything smooth." Five butlers: Popoff (Akim Tamiroff), Buzz Jenkins (Alan Mowbray), Emmett (Frank Jenks), Moreno (Sig Arno), and Reeves (Hans Conried) residing in the same building are attracted to Ann and their antics make for excellent comic routines. Produced by Flex Jackson and directed by Frank Borzage, this movie includes actors Walter Catlett, Evelyn Ankers, and Elsa Janssen, just to name a few. Look for Deanna Durbin's movie stand-in, Marie Osborne, acting as Mortimer Kalb's (Walter Catlett) secretary. The movie received one Academy Award nomination for Best Sound Recording.

An opening credit reading "The foods, drinks, clothes, shoes, rubber, gas and other articles consumed or used in this picture are purely imaginary and have no relation to any actual foods, drinks, clothes, shoes, rubber, gas and other articles of today, rationed or unrationed. Any resemblance is purely accidental. This is a fable of the day before yesterday," was a reminder that America was at war and such food items were not to be wasted. Conservation tactics were so high that in one scene a coffee cup appears on the verge of being dropped but is recovered without spilling a drop of the liquid as it appears the coffee is not liquified.

There were quite a few musical numbers. The Medley of Russian Songs (arranged by Max Rabinowitz sung in Russian by Deanna Durbin) and the featured song *None Shall Sleep* (Nessun Dorma from Turandot music by Giacomo Puccini sung in English by Deanna Durbin) being the most exceptional.

Variety magazine staff reviewed *His Butler's Sister* (December 31, 1942): "Despite tale's fragility, picture is brimful of light and amusing situations. Durbin is spotlighted with fine performance as the young and ambitious singer, getting sensitive direction under Frank Borzage." Sadly, as the movie arrived in theaters in December of 1943, Durbin saw her marriage to Paul end in divorce.

On February 7, 1944 *Lux Radio Theater* aired *His Butler's Sister*, where Deanna Durbin and Pat O'Brien reprised their movie roles with Robert Paige acting the character Charles Gerard (Franchot Tone in the movie). Paige was presented "as an upcoming new

Universal star" and "Deanna's next leading man." Paige also starred with Durbin in *Can't Help Singing*, her only full color film.

CHRISTMAS HOLIDAY
(July 31, 1944)

In 1943 producer Felix Jackson, who had worked with Pasternak and Foster in Europe, wanted to use the central points of W. Somerset Maugham's book *Christmas Holiday* (1939) and create an original story starring Deanna Durbin. The outline submitted, according to Richard Meryman in his book *Monk: The Wit, World and Life of Herman J. Mankiewicz* (New York William Morrow 1978 p279), originally told the tale of a "jilted soldier who travels to New York to kill his fiancé and her new boyfriend but meets Durbin's character along the way and gives up his murderous plans and returns to the army."

The scripting was given to veteran script writer Mankiewicz, who used Jackson's outline and Maugham's novel to develop a screenplay. He shifted the original Paris setting to America – specifically New Orleans and changed nearly everything else from the original outline. Joseph Greco wrote in his *The File on Robert Siodmak in Hollywood: 1941-1951* (Dissertation.com USA 1999) the screenplay "retains all the novel's tawdry edges, but by innuendo only." James Harvey, in his book *Movie Love in the Fifties* (Knopf Books, 2001), devoted an entire chapter to *Christmas Holiday*. Harvey wrote, "of course, the idea that innocence can be culpable is an insight that's at the heart of *noir* itself though rarely so clearly stated as here." p277. *Christmas Holiday* (1944) has been referred to as the bleakest film *noir* (pronounced n/war) of the 1940s. The term *"film noirs"* (French for "black film) was actually coined by French critic Nino Frank in 1946, so when *Christmas Holiday* was released there was no special genre to explain the casting of Gene Kelly and Deanna Durbin in such a sordid and dark film. Bosley Crowther, *New York Times* (June 29, 1944) reviewer noted: "The advancement of Deanna Durbin toward dramatic maturity is rather bluntly accelerated by Universal in the young star's new film – –"

Producer Jackson's choice of actor Gene Kelly (on loan from M.G.M.) and Deanna Durbin was a unique mix that worked very well! Kelly played Robert Manette the charming, yet murderous cad, while Deanna Durbin played dual roles: one, as Abigail Martin Manette and the other as Jackie Lamont. Durbin's characters were incredibly differed, Abigail being a naïve girl happily married to Robert, but who "becomes" Jackie a suffering wife and club hostess.

This tightly-scripted film under the expert control of director Robert Siodmak (pronounced as printed in all caps from a photograph of Siodmak's director chair, SEE-ODD-MACK) maneuvers the story through fanciful love and blissful marriage into crushed happiness and spiraling despair with the only glimmer of hope portrayed in the last scene of clouds separating to reveal stars. In *Movie Love in the Fifties* (previously cited) it is convincingly argued that Jackie/Abigail "is more alone than ever at the movie end."

Durbin gave an excellent performance against an extremely demanding role. She transforms from a naïve young girl, hopelessly in love, to a happy bride, then a disillusioned woman enduring redemptive suffering for the man she loves, who has been sentenced for a long term in prison for murder. It was reported that originally Durbin was called upon to portray a prostitute but balked and thus became a hostess/singer in a club, which appears to be a front for a brothel, which was the compromise. The shift in Durbin's character was deftly realized by giving her two movie names, Abigail Martin and Jackie Lamont. The Martin/Lamont story is revealed through a series of flashbacks told to newly commissioned Lieutenant Charles Mason (Dean Harens), who has literally dropped into the unfolding drama when his flight to San Francisco is forced to land in New Orleans due to inclement weather. Lt. Mason brings his own tale of woe; his planned Christmas wedding in San Francisco, cancelled via a telegram and his fiancée marrying someone else. He is determined to confront his ex-fiancée and the "done deed."

In New Orleans Lt. Mason is approached by newspaper-man Simon Fenimore (Richard Whorf) as a possible story lead about the forced landing. Fenimore, learning of Mason's destination plans, befriends the soldier and talks Mason into accompanying him to the club Maison de Fete. Fenimore convinces Mason the club owner Valerie De Merode (Gladys George) may be able to find alternate means for Lt. Mason to continue his journey. After introductions, Valerie tells the two men she cannot help. Simon, who is sort of a promoter for the club, asks Valerie to give him an advance on his weekly retainer. Jackie Lamont is called over to the table so Lt. Mason need not be alone. They clumsily attempt to dance and talk. Meanwhile Simon passes out, but not before giving Lt. Mason two seating passes for the Christmas Midnight Mass at the New Orleans's St. Louis Cathedral (note: the scene was actually filmed at St. Vibiana's Cathedral in Los Angeles which was closed in 1995 and reopened as a performing arts center in 2005). Jackie asks to go and when it appears Mason is apprehensive, entreats him to take her. The Mass becomes the catalyst for Jackie to break down and tell Mason a portion of her story – done as flashbacks. Jackie' vague answer to where she will stay the night when parting leads Mason to offer to find her a room in the hotel where he and other passengers are making their layover. Due to the holiday season, his and all other hotels in town are booked, so Jackie spends the night on the sofa in Mason's room, allowing Jackie to continue telling her story to Lt. Mason the next day. Lt. Mason cannot believe anyone would continue to love someone the way Jackie loves her wayward husband, con-vict, Robert Manette. He is, however, obviously impressed by the tale for after they depart each other's company, Mason decides to forget his revenge plans in California and return to New York. Later, while in the lobby, he learns from a newspaper headline that Robert Manette has escaped from jail. Lt. Mason goes to the club with a vague protective urge.

The hinge between Robert and Abigail is Robert's mother, Mrs. Manette (Gale Sondergaard), a tyrannical mother who dis-arms Abigail in their first meeting with her solicitous attitude and acceptance of the "love" between her son and Abigail. It doesn't take long for her actions to betray her true feelings toward Abigail and ultimately becomes a wedge between the two women. After the arrest and sentencing of Robert, Mrs. Manette's full fury is turned on Abigail. With a sharp slap to the face the mother blames her son's failure on Abigail's inability to change her son – which, she says, is the only reason she approved of their marriage.

According to Tony Thomas in his book *The Films of Gene Kelly* (The Citadel Press 1974), Gene Kelly said Deanna Durbin " '... considers this her best performance,' but Gene Kelly recalls her as being nervous and doubtful about it at the time, worrying that the public would not accept the dramatic change –".

Elliot Stein wrote in his *Village Voice* article "Robert Siodmak: 40s *Noir*" (May 2002), "Although audiences gasped in shock at the first sight of America's chirping child diva, heavily made up and in a décolleté gown in a sleazy club, *Christmas Holiday* was a money-spinner and Durbin has repeatedly cited it as her only worthwhile film." The audience did "gasp" and Durbin was heavily criticized for the Abigail/Jackie role. Under Siodmak's tight control and direction Durbin did not appear on screen until 20 minutes into the movie. Greco writes Siodmak's "... teasing approach is a brilliant touch" which was used to introduce "new" Durbin to her legion of fans. Both Greco and Harvey were impressed with Siodmak's approach and wrote in detail on this *mise en scène*. Greco, even in 1999, disagreed with the critics of the past: "Let me say this about Durbin's performance: it is by far the best of her career, owed much to Siodmak direction of her," and adds, "A young actress tackling a difficult role with intelligence and about as much audacity."

John Russell Taylor in his article in *Sight and Sound* magazine "Encounter with Siodmak" (Summer-Autumn 1959 p180-182) gave insight into how Siodmak viewed Durbin: "... she was difficult; she wanted to play a new part but flinched from looking like a tramp – – Still, she was quite effective, and oddly enough did very well."

Joseph Breen in a letter to Will Hays (August 1, 1944 from Greco cited p35) wrote: *Christmas Holiday* "tripled receipts of previous Durbin films – – *Christmas Holiday* was an 'unparalleled story' – – A thrill of dramatic intensity seldom, if ever, equaled on the screen." Strong words of praise from Breen, who was criticized for his strictness as administrator of the movie code, as well as the one who had originally turned the script down in 1939.

Author James Harvey (often cited) writes: *Christmas Holiday* was a "box office hit in many places tripling receipts of previous Durbin pictures – – It made a great deal of money, more than any other Durbin film had or would." *Variety* (July 26, 1944) reported, "*Christmas Holiday*, Deanna Durbin starrer, is reported topping all other Durbin productions in film rentals. On the basis of returns to date estimated that 'Holiday' will gross $2,250,000 to $2,600.000 domestics." Clive Hirschhorn (often cited) remarked on this one-time effort, "it was undeniably refreshing to see the studio's top money maker – – in a more substantially dramatic role."

And what is a Durbin fete without music. The theme music used to open and close the movie and the relationship between the star-crossed lovers is Wagner's *Tristan and Isolde*. When Durbin as Jackie first appears on the screen at the club she is viewed from the rear, walking to the bandstand where she sings Loesser's *Spring Will Be A Little Late This Year*. In happier moments as man and wife, Abigail sings Berlin's *Always*; later she will sing the same song prior to the final confrontation with the escaped Manette. Both songs reveal the destructive nature of blind love, the way it consumes the soul, and both are sung in a weary and bluesy manner at the club, much different from her light coloratura soprano operatic voice. The musical selection reinforces the bleakness of the film *noir* thriller (based in part on Dennis Schwartz 2004 review).

The film was nominated for one Academy Award; oddly enough for Best Scoring of a Dramatic or Comedy Picture.

Life magazine (July 3, 1944) did a spread on Durbin titled "Deanna Durbin: After 7 years of adolescent roles she becomes a mature dramatic star." She is photographed in the Brentwood home she and Paul built. Now single she lives with her sister Edith and Edith's son, "Dickie." One photograph shows her in the hallway with fan letters distributed neatly on the floor, with the cutline partially reading, "Since her initial success in *Three Smart Girls*, she has received an average of 16,000 letters monthly – – Deanna is Universal's most popular pin-up girl." There is a full-page essay and pictorial display on *Christmas Holiday*, with most of the photographs credited to photographer Ralph Crane or furnished by Universal. However, a single photograph by Philippe Halsman depicts a relaxed Deanna *sans* photo studio pose giving a rarely seen revealing and delightful photograph. Durbin talked about this photo in the 1983 David Shipman *Film and Filming* magazine (via several web sites) interview. "He (Halsman) said he was going to photograph me 'looking like and angel'. I answered that I may not know how I did want to be photographed, but if there was one way I certainly did not want to be photographed it was looking like an angel! He laughed and the picture he took more than satisfied me. I'll admit that for some of my public all this must have been hard to understand."

Prior to the release of *Can't Help Singing*, Durbin's photograph appeared in *Life* magazine (June 26, 1944) accompanying an article, "Movie Stand-Ins" (p49-51). The story detailed the life of a "stand-in" – those people who were hired to "relieve the stars of practically all duties except those of acting." The stand-ins "closely resemble the stars in coloring, build and movements" and "pose under the blazing lights while the camera crew runs out the tape to measure the distance from camera to nose and performs the endless details of focusing and light measurement which precedes the photographing of a sequence." The pay scale was low: $8.25 a day as compared to the $10.50 extras earned. However, it was mentioned that "with the bonuses and bit parts, the stand-in can average between $75 and $100 weekly." The short article concludes, "No stand-in has ever risen to stardom." Deanna Durbin's stand-in, Marie Osborne, is pictured with Durbin with the cutline reading: "Deanna Durbin and Marie Osborne have striking resemblance. In her fifth picture as Deanna's stand-in, Marie, who was baby star in silent (movies), plans movie comeback." Marie Osborne Yeats (November 5, 1911 – November 11, 2010) is considered, by some, to be the first major child star of

American silent films – billed simply as Baby Marie. She never made a major comeback but did perform in movies until the 50s when she began a new career as a costumer for western movies. She retired from movies in 1976. A read of her life is quite interesting – in many ways her story is akin to the modern day fairytale heroine Durbin 's early films described.

CAN'T HELP SINGING
(December 29, 1944)

The working title of *Can't Help Singing* (1944) was *Caro-line*, Deanna Durbin's character name in the movie. "According to Universal press materials, portions of the film were shot on location in Cedar City, Utah and Lake Arrowhead, California. A *Hollywood Reporter* news item also list Parowan Gap and other Utah locations as filming sites." (*American Film Institute Catalog of Feature Films, The first 100 years 1893-1993* online). It was to be the only Durbin movie filmed in glorious Technicolor and her only true musical. Most movie musicals of the 30s, 40s and 50s were light-hearted with songs interwoven into the narrative and *Can't Help Singing* was just that!

The movie opens with Cavalry Troops riding eastward to Washington D.C. to deliver the first shipment of gold ore from California during the California Gold Rush era. Caroline Frost (Durbin) is introduced singing the title song *Can't Help Sing-ing* (all music by Jerome Kern with lyrics by E.Y. Harburg) as she rides to the same destination in a two-horse carriage to meet her beau, Lieutenant Robert Lathan (David Bruce). Viewers are quickly made privy to the fact Caroline's father, Senator Martin Frost (Ray Collins) and her Aunt Cissy (Clara Blandick), do not approve of the relationship. Lt. Lathan's opportunistic conniving nature is demonstrated for the audience early in the show. In one of the most memorable lines in the movie Miss McLean (June Vincent) remarks to Layton, "You know the first time I saw you, you were riding in the park on a beautiful white steed. It was love at first sight. I'm convinced now it was the horse." Senator Frost announces to his daughter that Lt. Lathan's regiment has been sent to California to guard the rich Carstairs Mines. Deluded to think that this will end the romance, Frost goes to a party. However, Caroline heads west, but her naivety eventually finds

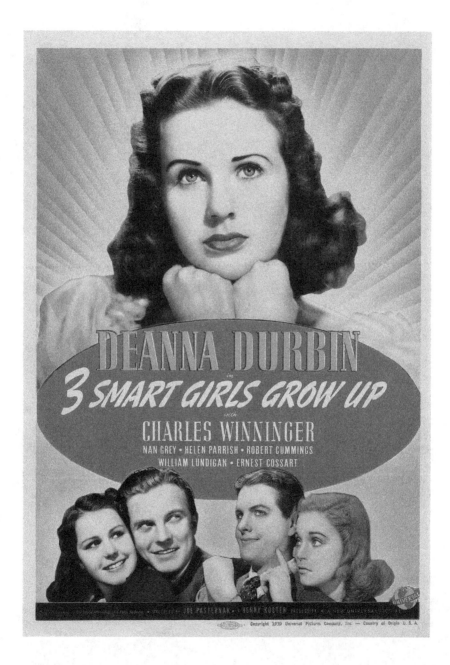

"That Certain Age," Deanna Durbin, Jackie Cooper and Peggy Stewart.

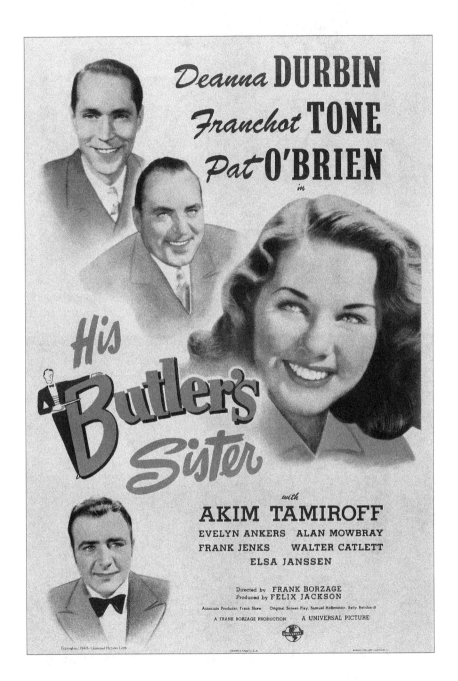

"Christmas Holiday," Richard Whorf, Dean Harens, Gladys George, Deanna Durbin and Gene Kelly.

"Something in the Wind"

Youthful Deanna Durbin, 1939.

Joe Pasternak and Deanna Durbin, 1940.

James Durbin, Deanna Durbin and Ada Durbin, 1944.

Deanna Durbin and Vaugh Paul wedding April 18, 1941.

Felix Jackson and Deanna Durbin wedding, 1945.

Charles David and Deanna Durbin on the set of Lady on A Train, 1945.

Deanna Durbin and daughter Jessica, 1947.

Deanna Durbin and son Peter, 1952.

her in the covered wagon train party with Johnny Lawler (Robert Paige), whom Caroline has promised $10,000, paid on reaching California by wealthy gold mine owner, Jake Carstairs (Thomas Gomez), for having brought him his "fiancé," Caroline. Beautiful scenery, beautiful music, (especially *Any Moment Now*, sung against the background of Bryce Canyon, Utah) and misadventures fill in the miles to California. Prince Gregory Stroganosky (Akim Tamiroff) and his servant Koppa (Leonid Kinskey) add a touch of humor, especially Gregory's foil as Caroline's husband so they can travel with the covered wagon convoy. Ultimately, even though Carstairs gets the last laugh, Lawler gets the girl!

Bosley Crowther in his *New York Times* review (December 26, 1944) writes "...the costumes and scenery are dazzling – in opulent color don't forget – and the songs, as we say, are fair reason for taking time off to see the show. Jerome Kern is the author of them, and they range from the lyrical title song to a rousing choral number called 'Californ-i-ay.'" Durbin's wardrobe is surprisingly luxurious, especially for a cross-country adventure. For the closing number she wears two different gowns.

It is the fourth film produced by Felix Jackson and the second directed by Frank Ryan. *Can't Help Singing* received two Academy Award nominations|: Best Music, Song – *More and More* (Jerome Kern, E.Y. Harbug) and Best Scoring of a Musical Picture (Jerome Kern, H.J. Salter).

"According to a *HR* (*Hollywood Reporter*) news items, Universal originally sought Rouben Mamoulian as director, because he had directed the successful Broadway musical *Oklahoma*. (*American Film Institute Catalog of Feature Films, The first 100 years 1893-1993* often cited).

Variety (July 12, 1944 p21) reported *Can't Help Singing* carried a "budget of $2,600,000, highest the company (Universal) has ever had." According to *HR* (*Hollywood Reporter*), the film's $300,000 advertising budget was the largest of any Universal film to date (*American Film Institute Catalog of Feature Films, The first 100 years 1893-1993* often cited).

In January 28, 1945 the British Edition of *Yank*, the Army weekly magazine, named Deanna Durbin as "Pin up Girl" and honored her with a full-page photograph.

Shortly after *Can't Help Singing*'s premiere and a few months before the release of *Lady on a Train*, Deanna Durbin and Universal producer, Felix Jackson, were married – June 13, 1945.

LADY ON A TRAIN
(December 29, 1945)

Lady on a Train (1945) has been aptly described as a film *noir* comedy, and with the broad definition of film *noir* it fits. With the critical backlash of Deanna Durbin's role in *Christmas Holiday*, *Lady on a Train* appears to have been an attempt to satisfy the critics while starring Durbin in a dramatic, suspenseful thriller with a touch of humor. This witty screenplay was scripted by Edmund Beloin and Robert O'Brien from an original story by Leslie Charteris. The first page of a script, dated August 21, 1943 by Leslie Charteris, became the opening scene in the movie, including the interior shot of a Pullman train car. In the script "Judy Lane" is described as reading a novel with a "lurid jacket" titled "Lady on a Train by Leslie Charteris." (Boston University Howard Gotlieb Archival Research Center holds the draft of the Charteris script). The final script credited to Beloin and O'Brien appears to have largely followed the original Charteris work as his expanded version was published as a 25¢ paperback novelette (Shaw Press copyrighted by Universal Pictures, Inc. 1945) following the filming. Charteris is best known for his mystery stories, especially "The Saint" series.

Durbin never looked so beautiful - and with the variety of outfits she wore throughout the film, she never looked more glamorous on camera. The movie opens at night with the haunting sounds of a train entering the railyards as music sustains the feeling of suspense and expectations. The moviegoers are introduced to Nikki Collins (Durbin) eating bon-bons and reading a mystery novel, *The Case of the Headless Bride* by Wayne Morgan. A pensive but casual glance out the train window and Nikki is witness to a murder being committed; the stage is set for a "whodunit" mystery. Arriving from San Francisco, she is met by Mr. Haskell (Edward Everett Horton) who attempts to get Nikki settled. Agitated by what she has seen Nikki reports the murder to the police. However, when Sergeant Christe (William Frawley) determines, after Nikki brandishes the mystery book she was reading on the train, she is just imaging a whodunit mystery and dismisses her with the suggestion she get the mystery writer to help her find the killer. And so, she does! On learning from a movie newsreel, the murdered man's name, Josiah Waring (Thurston Hall), Nikki decides to do some snooping at the Waring mansion and finds herself trapped in the room where the will is being read. She is mistaken to be Margo Martin, singer at the Circus nightclub, and Josiah's mistress and a major benefactor of the will. Now with mystery writer Wayne Morgan (David Bruce) in tow, one misadventure after another ensues. Romance and song, especially the steamy *Give Me a Little Kiss*, coupled with macabre settings laced with humor, make for a madcap adventure. Suffice to say, Nikki does stumble onto the killer.

Durbin is supported by Ralph Bellamy, Dan Duryea, Maria Palmer, George Coulouris, Allen Jenkins, Samuel S. Hinds, Ben Carter, Jacqueline deWit, and Elizabeth Patterson. Look for future western star, Alfred Wilson "Lash" LaRue in a speaking role as a waiter dressed as a clown.

This was another production for Felix Jackson, this time with Charles David as director. The Academy Awards nominated the film for Best Sound, Recording.

Moments after Nikki views the murder from her Pullman car window, she goes in search of a conductor. The unexpected dialogue between Nikki and train conductor (Chester Clute) is humorous and well-acted through facial expressions and body movements and perfect comic timing.

> Nikki: "Conductor if we entered this tunnel at 9:17 – I mean 12:13 – My watch is still on San Francisco time – And the rails go click-click every 2½ seconds – See? Click-click. We've crossed one now. And each rail is 21 feet long – anyway at 9:11– that is in San Francisco – it is 12:13 here. It is 12:14 now. Where were we?"
>
> Conductor: "Well, I was on my way to the baggage car."

The *New York Times* (September 15, 1945) reviewer Bosley Crowther slammed the movie with his opening remarks, "The sooner Deanna Durbin and her producers realize that she is not a dramatic actor nor even a fair farceuse, the sooner we'll all be spared the bother of such embarrassments as 'Lady on a Train.'" Crowther's entire review runs in this vein, even to personal remarks regarding Durbin's weight. Fortunately, current reviews of the movie are favorable.

Deanna Durbin enjoyed a rather unusual "first" as annotated in a cutline on the back of a Universal photograph, dated November 5, 1945 for publications in newspapers. The cutline read in part: "Just before breaking a bottle of champagne for the christening, Deanna Durbin is congratulated by George Kelly, vice president of Pullman Co., upon being the first screen star to have a Pullman named for her." Participating was George B. Hansen, an agent of the Southern Pacific Railroad.

The year 1946 is considered as one of the best in cinema's history. In the United States alone the average weekly attendance was 90 million. And this even though the average price of tickets had increased from 23¢ in 1936 to 40¢ in 1946. The increase of movie production during the war years had included many movies produced to satisfy the "anything goes" taste. Now, with the ticket cost increase, studios had to make carefully crafted movies to bring the audience to the theater.

1946 was also a memorable year for Deanna Durbin but for an entirely different reason – on February 7, 1946 Deanna and Felix welcomed their first child, a girl they named Jessica Louise Jackson.

Universal Pictures experienced a corporate upheaval in November 12, 1946 with a merger which resulted in a new company name – Universal-International – a new logo and new strategic direction. The new Universal-International production head issued a directive to the various departments that no feature film would run under 70 minutes, no "B" movies were to be started, all serials were halted, no more formula westerns and more Technicolor.

BECAUSE OF HIM
(January 18, 1946)

When *Because Of Him* (1946) was released the *New York Times* panned the movie giving all acting credit to Charles Laughton. The movie opens with the final showing at the Mercury Theater of *Cyrano de Bergerac* starring flamboyant John Sheridan (Charles Laughton). Kim Walker (Durbin) is first viewed at the stage door attempting to get Sheridan's autograph, on a trifold falsified letter of introduction to theatrical producer Charles Gilbert (Stanley Ridges). She does get Sheridan's autograph, but even more importantly garners the attention of Gilbert and Sheridan. The following day, on the way to Gilbert's office, she encounters Paul Taylor (Franchot Tone), who performs an elaborate ruse of rescuing Kim from getting hit by a car all just to get her phone number. She brushes him off when she sees through his deception. Later, at the meeting with Gilbert, she "meets" Paul and learns, much to her chagrin, he is a famous playwright. The movie takes many twists and turns, and a hint of romantic entanglement is brought on by the songs sung by Kim. For John it is a highly emotional *Danny Boy* while for Paul it is with *Good Bye!* (Francesco Tosti and G. J. Whyte-Melville). They are all drawn together in Paul's new play, "Strange Laughter." In a moment of jealousy, Paul has his name removed from the marquee. However, at the opening, Paul, slinking outside, overhears remarks during intermission praising the show and Kim's acting. All does end well.

It was produced by Felix Jackson and directed by Richard Wallace.

The *New York Times* (January 25, 1946) reviewer Bosley Crowther praises Laughton, "Although Deanna Durbin gets the top billing in Because of Him, the picture . . . unquestionably belongs to Charles Laughton." He includes in his review his apparent pet peeve, "It is becoming increasingly evident that the lady has severe limitations as an actress, and the sooner the wise minds at Universal recognize this fact, the happier we all will be." However, in a moment of praise he concludes with, "But the fact which can't be stressed too strongly is that Miss Durbin should make the most of her greatest asset - her voice."

On the other hand, *Variety* (December 31, 1945) review reads, "Film is a merry mélange of music, comedy and drama with a good story and a top cast. Durbin, even though she portrays a stage-struck waitress through most of the plot, is gowned to perfection and looks ditto. Music plays a minor part in the film, with the star's vocal efforts limited to three songs, but seldom has she been in finer voice."

Rumors of Deanna Durbin's dissatisfaction with Hollywood and acting begin to circulate again.

I'LL BE YOURS
(February 2, 1947)

I'll Be Yours (1947) was a remake of Preston Sturges' cinematic rewrite of Ferenc Molnar's screenplay, *The Good Fairy*, with the new adaptations by Felix Jackson and with additional songs. This film stars Durbin as Louise Ginglebuster, who comes from such a small town the New York train nearly passes the station as she waits - reversing to pick her up. Louise meets George Prescott (Tom Drake on loan from M.G.M.) after the wind blows her hat off. Later she learns his name as she attempts – with a most delightful comedy skit between Wechsberg and Ginglebuster – to eat an inexpensive meal at a restaurant managed by Wechsberg (William Bendix). Wechsberg dreams of owning his own fancy restaurant so George, a struggling attorney, negotiates his meals in exchange for his legal expertise. His only apparent ambition is to be honest, which has kept him poor! Once the zany antics of Louise begin, wealth is within George's grasp, as wealthy meat packer J. Conrad Nelson (Adolphe Menjou), dazzled by Louise's beauty, makes a play for her only to learn she is "married" to George. Meanwhile George, also smitten by Louise, becomes involved with Nelson through Louise's "little white lie" when he is approached by Nelson to represent his firm. George now has steady work. Meanwhile Louise, wanting to rectify the "lie" that she is "married," attempts to unravel the situation – only to make matters worse. Once again, however, all ends well!

The soundtrack songs, especially the thrilling version of *Granada* (written by Agustin Lara), *It's Dream Time* (lyrics by Jack Brooks, music by Walter Schumann), *Love's Own Sweet Song* (*Sari Waltz* lyrics by Catherine Cushing and E. P. Heath, music by Emmerich Kalman) and *Cobbleskill School Song* (lyrics Jack Brooks, music by Walter Schumann, sung by Deanna Durbin and Walter Catlett) – Walter Catlett plays Mr. Buckingham, owner of Buckingham Theater where Louise finds employment as an usherette – add to this lively comedy.

The *New York Times* review of February 22, 1947 authored by T.M.P. does not have the harsher tones of previous *Times* reviews by Crowther and reads: "Miss Durbin is in fine voice and she again brings all of her vast and appealing girlish charm to the role of a small town innocent – –" concludes with, " ... *I'll be Yours* manages to be pleasant, thanks mostly to Miss Durbin."

Produced by Felix Jackson and directed by William A. Seiter.

A photograph from the set of *I'll Be Yours* on Turner Classic Movie website capturing Deanna Durbin in a Pullman holding a baby solicited the following email from Sylvia Corbett. Sylvia emailed November 21, 2016: "I was the baby in this movie with Deanna Durbin. I have an autographed photo of myself with Deanna in a scene on a train. She is singing to me. I was too little to remember it, but I'm glad to have the photos and letter from the studio. There were also newspaper articles and ads. The scenes on the train were cut from the final version of the movie, but I'm hoping that someday you will produce a DVD with all the original footage if it's still out there somewhere." There were several, differently posed, photographs of Deanna and the baby distributed by Universal promoting the movie, I'll Be Yours.

SOMETHING IN THE WIND
(July 21, 1947)

Something in the Wind (1947) opens with radio disc jockey Mary Collins (Durbin) singing *The Turntable Song* as she prepares to sign off the air. Mary is told someone is waiting to see her in the hallway and thinking it might be regarding a sponsor for her radio show, she happily approaches Donald Read (John Dall). Read, however is not the bearer of good news and informs her, in no uncertain terms, the regular financial arrangement paid her in the past and stated in his will to continue by his late wealthy grandfather must cease. Mary, who would receive a cash settlement, need but sign a form releasing the estate from further obligations. In a scene demonstrative of Durbin's comic timing, both verbally and physically, feisty Mary tells Read off. With a quick downward sweep, she snatches at the legal document, misses it and without hesitation repeats the action, tearing the document up, while telling him to "get out." With poise, she turns smartly and leaves. Durbin is beautiful with a new feather cut hairdo and dressed in a simple but attractive outfit. Her hat brim is pulled down smartly to reveal only one eye, which sparkles when she thinks Read might be a sponsor and glares with contempt when confronted with the arrogance of Read. Momentarily foiled, John, together with his grandmother, Grandma Read (Margaret Wycherly), and his third cousin, Charlie Read (Donald O'Connor), scheme to get her to sign. Mary learns from her aunt, Mary Collins (Jean Adair), who raised her niece, that it was she who had been receiving the payments. The elderly Mary had been a governess in the Read household caring for the children of the late Henry Read's sister. She and Henry fell in love, but the social differences forced them apart and he married someone else. Feeling guilty Henry had been sending a monthly allowance which allowed Mary's aunt to raise her niece. Grandma Read, annoyed that John had failed to settle the matter, demands Mary be brought to the house so to finalize the matter. John and Charlie ploy to kidnap Mary.

Once this takes place the story turns and spins out of control. Uncle Chester Read (Charles Winninger) and Donald's fiancée, Charissa Prentice (Helena Carter), added additional complications. Donald, in an effort to talk with Mary privately, uses an exuberant song and dance routine, *I Love a Mystery*, to accost Mary with the fact he knows of her ruse. Finally, he reveals a stack of checks written twenty years ago when she was a child, but he throws them in the fire. Together they conspire for separate reasons; Mary to get even with the high-handed manners of the Read family and Charlie, who secretly loves Clarisa, for a scandal which might threaten Donald's relationship with Clarisa. So, the charade begins. Mary agrees to a settlement for herself but raises the ante high with the casual remark of there being a "baby." The delightful humorous antics eventually becomes heartbreak as the bygone past is relived. Donald and Mary fall in love! Grandmother Mrs. Read takes a hand in creating a major derailment but eventually resolution is achieved!

The New York Times review by Abe Weiler, August 29, 1947, made favorable comments about Durbin: "The ebullient, girlish Deanna Durbin of old is back again in *Something in the Wind*, to warm the hearts of her fans and the corporate soul of her movie mentors, Universal- International."

All the songs had lyrics by Leo Robin and music by Johnny Green, except the operatic selection *Miserere* by Verdi, a solo by Durbin and jail guard Tony (Jan Peerce). Peerce, a tenor who so impressed maestro Arturo Toscanini he was chosen to sing leading operatic roles on the conductor's radio broadcasts and recordings. Peerce made his debut with the Metropolitan Opera Company on November 29, 1941 singing Alfredo in *La Traviata* from which *Miserere* is taken. Johnny Green can be seen as the bandleader at the fashion show, who asked Mary to sing *You Wanna Keep Your Baby Looking Right*.

Reviewer Weiler summed it up well: "All in all, entertainment is the word for *Something in the Wind*."

Look for the quartet, The Four Williams Brothers, with a youthful Andy Williams, backing O'Connor in both *The Turntable Song* and the title song, *Something in the Wind*.

This film marked the first time Deanna Durbin worked with producer Joseph Sistrom and director Irving Pichel.

According to several sources, Martha Shearer (*New York City and the Hollywood Musical* 2016) and Hisato Masuyama (liner notes of the *Up in Central Park* CD – Sepia 2012) Universal-International acquired rights to two movies for Deanna Durbin, *Song of Norway* and *Up in Central Park*. *Central Park* was to begin shooting in December 1946 as a Technicolor production, co-starring Vincent Price and Dick Haymes, one of the most popular male singers at the time. The musical was placed under the direction of Johnny Green (composer of songs in *Something in the Wind*). There are several arguments why this lavish production did not happen. A strike in late 1946 by the Technicolor processing facilities caused the project to be postponed until 1947. In September 28, 1947 the *New York Times* reported the new owners of Universal-International, which were merged July 30, 1946, were engaging in a cost-saving measure keeping budgets low and filming only "those stories that promised high US box-office returns." There were songs removed from the original theatrical musical, new songs written and one borrowed, *Pace, Pace Mio Dio* (from the opera *La Forza del Destino* music by Giuseppe Verdi, libretto by Francesco Maria Piave), and when the movie was released in July 1948 five songs had been cut from the finished film. For years Deanna Durbin fans assumed the number was three; however, with the 2012 release of Sepia's soundtrack CD, it was revealed five songs, entirely or partially, had been cut.

UP IN CENTRAL PARK
(July 1948)

Up in Central Park (1948) was based on a Broadway musical by the same title that opened in January 27, 1945 at the Century Theatre and closing June 10, 1945 after 504 performances. The show continued at the Broadway Theatre, June 11 through April 13, 1946 and later revived at the City Center between May 19 and May 30, 1947. The original story written by Herbert and Dorothy Fields with music by Sigmund Romberg is centered around the corruption in New York City under the reins of William M. "Boss" Tweed, who played a major role in New York City and State politics in the 19th century. Karl Tunberg, who directed the movie, was also responsible for the movie script. The movie is a light-hearted romantic musical that makes no attempt to convey the historic aspect of that era, but Rosie Moore (Durbin) does have the opportunity to chide "Boss" Tweed (Vincent Price) with a mild reprehend, repel his romantic interest and leave his life as the Tweed's Tammany Hall political machine falls. The movie opens with the rousing political mayoral election rally, spelling out the corruption of Tammany Hall, the Democratic Party-political machine. Rosie is introduced as an immigrant arriving on a liner to New York City with her dad, Timothy Moore (Albert Sharpe), bursting with pride on arriving in America to the tune of *Oh Say, Can You See (What I See)*. Tim, for voting 23 times as a dead man, is paid $50.00. It is at this juncture "Boss" Tweed meets and becomes enraptured with Tim's beautiful daughter and appoints her father park commissioner. Enters John Matthews (Dick Haymes), a young idealistic and ambitious newspaper reporter who, too, is smitten by Rosie. The conflict between John wanting to expose the corruption of "Boss" Tweed and Rosie's naïve belief in Tweed's goodness complicates John and Rosie's relationship. But good triumphs - and so does John and Rosie!

The director for *Up in Central Park* was veteran director William A. Seiter.

It is reported of all the 21 films Deanna Durbin made only two: *Up in Central Park*, and *For the Love of Mary* were her only box-office disappointments.

FOR THE LOVE OF MARY
(September 1, 1948)

September 1, 1948 marks the date for the release of Deanna Durbin's last movie, *For the Love of Mary* (1948). *For the Love of Mary* had been announced in 1946 as Durbin's next film but it had to be shelved and wasn't released until after *Up in Central Park*. A *Time* magazine (Monday, October 11, 1948) reviewer called it a "a plot heavy little picture with a deceptively simple beginning." Mary Peppertree (Durbin), a telephone operator in Washington, D.C., changes job, moving from the Supreme Court switchboard to the White House switchboard, and finds herself involved with an aggressive ichthyologist (the branch of zoology dealing with fishes), David Paxton (Dan Taylor). A comical tetra angle of romance and confusion with Mary's former fiancé Phillip Manning (Jeffery Lynn), Navy Lieutenant Tom Farrington (Edmond O'Brien), and David Paxton. Lt. Farrington is engaged to a powerful newspaper owner/editor's daughter who is not too happy with the state of affairs and threatens to make things tough for the administration through his newspaper. The ichthyologist situation involves Paxton owning a Pacific island to which he cannot return to continue his fish research because the Navy Department has restricted the island. And then there are Mary's hiccups! It seems whenever Mary is emotionally stressed, she hiccups. Only one of the three kisses from her suitors causes her to hiccup. No spoilers here: you will have to watch the film to learn who it is! Throughout the whirlwind of activity Gustav Heindel (Hugo Haas), owner of Gustav Restaurant, where much of the action takes place, is tutored by the Supreme Court Justices for his American citizenship test. As the situation regarding the U.S. Government, Paxton and his atoll, swirls to a climax, all involved are gathered at the restaurant where a party is planned to celebrate Gustav's new status as an American citizen. Unfortunately, the festivities are cancelled due to the fact Gustav failed the test by not completing it in the allotted time. Paxton detained because he was an American citizen – is to be deported. This complicates the matter – it forces the U. S. Government to accept all his demands. Finally, when the U. S. Navy negotiates for the purchase of the island to save the naval base, Paxton agrees to sell on several conditions – Philip be made a judge in a court at least 1,500 miles from Washington, Lieutenant Farrington be given sea duty, and all persons on the island be declared citizens of America – and as Gustav had been declared a citizen of the island by decree of Paxton, he would now be an American citizen.

A *Time* magazine (October 11, 1948) review summarizes the convoluting events nicely: "From there on, the plot begins to prove how intricate a plot can get; before it's over, practically all the brass and big-wiggery in Washington is standing helplessly on its ear – all, more or less, for the love of Mary. The mere fantastic nimbleness of the story is rather amusing, carried along at a good reckless clip."

The "intricate plot" was supported by an array of character actors including: Ray Collins, Harry Davenport, Morris Ankrum, and Louise Beavers to name a few.

The songs ranged from old favorites *Moonlight Bay*, *I'll Take You Home Again, Kathleen*, *Let Me Call You Sweetheart* (not sung by Durbin), a Johann Strauss' song, *On the Wings of a Song*, adaption by Edgar Fairchild with lyrics by Sidney Miller, and a charming version of the male's role, with Deanna Durbin wearing a moustache made from tree greenery, of *Largo al factotum* from The *Barber of Seville* by Rossini.

The standard *It's a Big, Wide, Wonderful World* (music and lyrics by John Rox), sung by Deanna Durbin, was cut from the film. The cut footage was included in the VHS-tape release from Universal.

Original screenplay was by Oscar Brodney, with Robert Arthur as producer and Frederick de Cordova as director.

A *New York Times* review by Bosley Crowther (September 23, 1948) declares the movie *For the Love of Mary* to be "a sly piece of propaganda against the administrators of our government in

Washington." Continuing his review in this manner he concludes with, "And for all the obvious things that have been done to make Miss Durbin seem entrancing to an assortment of old and young men, such as sing a few songs and smile sublimely, it still seems a sly political plot. Who could be behind it? Universal-International? Investigate!" Leaves one to believe the entry review was tongue in cheek.

The *Bakersfield Californian* (August 21, 1948 p4) published an article that Universal-International was suing Deanna Durbin in the amount of "$87,000 – alleging Miss Durbin was indebted to it (the studio) for the amount." A studio spokesman acknowledged the "dispute arose over salary paid the actress when on leave." (October 1941-January 1942)

The *New York Times* (August 23, 1948) filed a similar report, with the figure in the lawsuit to be $87,083 in wages paid her in advance. In the June 19, 1949 issue the *New York Times* reported Durbin settled the complaint amicably by agreeing to star in three more pictures, including one to be shot on location in Paris. However, the studio allowed her contract to expire on August 31, 1949. Durbin choose to retire and Universal-International paid her $200,000 severance pay.

Before *For the Love of Mary,* was released, September 1, 1949, it was reported by Thomas Brady in his column "Hollywood Digest" in the *New York Times* (June 19, 1949) that Universal-International announced due to "increasing viewers apathy" it was paying Durbin the salary due her for the three remaining movies in her contract and releasing her from the contract.

According to various sources Pasternak wanted her to sign at M.G.M., where he headed a film unit since leaving Universal in 1942. In Pasternak's book *Easy the Hard Way* (often cited p183), he concludes his chapter on Durbin with, "Greatness does not fall from a true star like a cloak. It is in the very marrow and bones of their being. One day, I hope she will call me and say, quite simply, 'Joe, I'm ready.' That will be all I need to know."

Though it was rumored only a few months after the birth of daughter Jessica (February 7, 1946) the Jacksons separated and eventually divorced on October 27, 1949.

In a *Los Angeles Times* (April 25, 1982) article, "On the Trail of Deanna" by David Paskvo, it was reported Deanna Durbin "secretly" married Charles Henri David on December 21, 1950 in his home town of Sarreguemines, on the Saar River, near Metz in eastern France, and the couple - with Durbin's daughter, Jessica - moved to Neauphle-le-Chateau commune (administrative division), 35 miles outside Paris. On July 2, 1951 a son, Peter Henry, was born to the couple. Peter was Deanna's second child and Charles' third.

And "poof" . . . no more Deanna Durbin movies, recordings or public appearances; just home life and travel, with her husband and two children.

AFTERWARDS

Even as Deanna Durbin's Hollywood star fades, her decades in the movies retain their worldwide impact. Anne Frank, during her years in hiding, pasted pictures of celebrities cut from movie magazines over her bed. In the documentary film *Anne Frank Remembered* (1995), Deanna Durbin's picture is pointed out by Frank's friend Hannah Pick-Goslar.

Pat Herman claimed his 1958 interview was the first interview with Deanna Durbin since moving to France and marrying; however, *Parade* magazine printed a story in its July 1, 1956 issue under the heading *Whatever happened to Deanna Durbin?* by *Parade* West Coast Correspondent Lloyd Shearer, datelined Neauphle-le-Chateau, France. The copy viewed was from the *Augusta Chronicle* (July 1, 1956 Sunday insert p18). A near complete article is reproduced here to show how similar both were in depicting a glimpse of Deanna Durbin's life in the mid-50s.

"Remember Deanna Durbin, the little girl who sang like an angel?

Remember how single-handedly she lifted Universal Pictures out of the red by starring in 10 consecutive box-office hits? That series began back in 1936, with *Three Smart Girls*. Ten years later, at 23, Deanna was earning $200,000 a year but feeling pretty unhappy about it all. Not long after that, she was out of pictures.

You'd hardly recognize Deanna today. Matter of fact, she wouldn't give you the chance. Despite all the material gain it brought her, she wants desperately to forget her 'unnatural Hollywood childhood fame.' Now 33 she lives serenely in this small village outside Paris. She lives with her third husband, film director Charles Henri David and her two children, Jessica (by her second husband Felix Jackson) and Peter, the small son of her present marriage.

Their home is an old dilapidated farmhouse around which the grass grows uncut and the roses bloom full and thorny. Deanna does her own housework, her own shopping, once a week brings in a maid for the heavy cleaning.

She refuses to see people from Hollywood or newsmen who drive down from Paris for a pleasant chat. The villages have been instructed to answer all queries concerning her with, 'I'm sorry there is no Mademoiselle Durbin here.' They lie with straight and convincing faces.

Does she grow lonely?

'Hardly ever,' her tall bespectacled husband told me. 'We have close friends and Deanna has her music teacher. Yes, she still takes singing lessons. Her voice, I think, is more beautiful than ever. She practices two, maybe three hours a day, but when she sings now, it is for the family. Here in the country she is not bothered by agents, columnists, big deals. Here she has a chance to lead a normal life, something she never knew in Hollywood.'

Will she ever make another movie? 'That is hard to tell,' M. David said. 'I am sure that for a girl who has known such tremendous success there must be at least a little longing for the past.' Lloyd Shearer has a baker to argue the point of why would she care about the past. The baker is quoted as saying, 'Today she is happy and gay. A little fat perhaps – –' Shearer concludes with, 'So – if she wants it that way and is happy that way, then *that is whatever happened to Deanna Durbin*'. The article is illustrated with two photographs, one showing a current candid shot of Deanna Durbin, her husband and son "shopping in an open market." The other a posed photograph of Deanna Durbin's first on screen kiss from Robert Stack in *First Love* in 1939.

In the March 6, 1958 p16 of the *The Desert Sun* newspaper, a weekly – at the time – serving the Palm Springs, California community there appeared, what the author claimed to be, the first interview with Deanna Durbin since moving to France and marrying Charles David. The article – under the title *Deanna Durbin Still Sings - At Home in France* by Pat Herman, United Press Staff Correspondent discloses a slice of life during their self-imposed privacy. Datelined Neauphle - Le - Chateau, France (UP) – "Remember Deanna Durbin? Well she is now a happy French housewife who says nothing could lure her back to Hollywood.

Still a beautiful brunette, though heavier than in her film days, the 34-year-old Deanna says for the first time in her life she is enjoying privacy with her family. 'And I would not change it for the world.' she said. Deanna ended a 13-year movie career in 1949 to marry French film director Charles David and retire to this village of 958 people less than 30 miles from Paris. Her talk with me was her first interview since then. 'I was never happy making pictures,' she said. 'They never allowed me to grow up as a normal child.' Mme. David said she has determined to spare her daughter, 11-year-old Jessica, and her son, Peter, 6, a similar childhood. 'Some movie stars say this but don't mean it,' said her distinguished-looking 51-year-old husband. 'But in my wife's case, the 'no' on publicity is definite.' The Davids live in a two-story farmhouse surrounded by a high stone wall. The local garageman across the road tips them off when 'uninvited guests' are seen in the vicinity. Deanna still practices – one hour every morning. 'Now I can sing whatever I like,' said the actress who once made $150,000 a picture. 'But the most exciting thing at the moment is Peter studying piano. We go into Paris once a week for lessons. He is not yet in the Mozart stage, but I get a tremendous kick out of singing with him to help him practice.' Deanna drives the family car and does most of her own shopping in nearby markets. The shopkeepers respect her as a canny bargainer and the butcher says he is sure she is a good cook. She and her husband still make frequent trips to Paris to go the theater and dinner parties. She plans to visit her parents, Mr. and Mrs. James Durbin of North Hollywood, this summer."

On a second read of these two articles, maybe the one by Pat Herman is the first interview as Deanna Durbin is quoted throughout, whereas the *Parade* item by Lloyd Shearer does not quote Deanna at all. It reminded me of a *Parents' Magazine* article (November 1940 p72) with the reporter writing, ". . . And while tiny gentle Mrs. Durbin received me graciously and showed me – –" Here listing items of Deanna's concluding with "– – no reporter ever interviews Deanna in her home." In the 1956 interview above you get the same feeling. The interviewer is not talking to Deanna, but with her husband Charles, who is graciously responding to the questions.

Deanna Durbin was inducted onto Hollywood's Walk of Fame, February 8, 1960.

In 1980, just for an instant, Deanna Durbin was in the "public eye." In the May issue of *Life* magazine (p24) there was printed a photograph of a perky attractive 59-year-old Deanna Durbin holding a copy of the February 1980 issue of *Life* (with Mickey Rooney on the cover) and a letter from Durbin under the heading *Lost Star Found*: "I may have stopped being a movie star, but I'm still a ham at heart – proof being the enclosed photo, the latest snapshot my husband took of me. If you care to publish it, it might set straight the false rumors about my figure. These, after so many years of happy oblivion, still disturb me a little and are not compensated by that first sentence of old friends when meeting me, 'Deanna! But you're not at all plump!' No, I can still pass under the Arc de Triomphe without holding my breath." Closing with her full name Deanna Durbin David, Neauphle-le-Château, France. The photo has a cutline simply reading "Deanna Durbin today" – – "poof" she was gone again!

An interesting testament to Deanna's popularity was a story told by Margaret Sams. Sams and her young son were placed in a Japanese internment camp after the bombing of a Naval Base in Cavite, a province in the Philippines located on the southern shores of Manila Bay, on December 10, 1941. From this experience Sams wrote the book *Forbidden Family: A Wartime Memoir of the Philippines, 1941-1945* (edited by Lynn Z. Bloom, published by University of Wisconsin Press, Madison, WI 1989), in which she described her detention and of the other 2,000 civilians who had the misfortune of being captured as well. Sams wrote in detail of the psychological tricks the Japanese used to intimidate, demoralize and demean the prisoner's hope of escape or liberation. One example of this was, during the first hectic week of interment, the prisoners were given a flyer which they read with great sorrow and horror of Deanna Durbin's death! It was reported it was a horrific death suffered while giving birth. Durbin's "death," at the height of her fame in 1941, was so devastating even to those in the midst of the agonizing experience of being prisoners, that all mourned her "death." The prisoners even held a memorial service in her honor. Later, one of the men at the camp, Jerry Sams (who would become Margaret Sams husband after their liberation), built a one tube radio and he was able to pick-up a San Francisco radio station. On Christmas Eve 1944, while listening for news, he jerked off his earphones and pressed them to Margaret's ear. She heard a woman's voice announcing herself as Deanna Durbin and dedicating the evening program of music to the women of the Philippines. Years later after the publication of her book, in 1997, Margaret located Deanna Durbin David's address and sent her a letter. Deanna was so moved she responded, requesting a copy of the book, and described the book as: "It was written by someone whom I consider a very dear friend." The entire story of the Los Baños Internment Camp and the lightning swift rescue efforts in 1945 is an exciting story of bravery, determination and heroic actions on the part of both internees and liberators.

Deanna's legion of fans remained faithful throughout her retirement. The BBC (British Broadcasting Corporation) reported that over the past four decades consistently more requests have been submitted for Durbin's films and music than for those of any other Hollywood Golden Age movie and singing star. Even into the 1990s Durbin's VHS releases of her films by MCA/UNIVERSAL were bestsellers – being the most sold videos of the "Classics" series, which included videos by Crosby, Dietrich, Colbert, etc. Patrons of various public television stations tuned in to enjoy and support public broadcasting as they aired her films as a part of fundraising efforts during the 1980s and early 1990s.

From various sources one gathers Deanna and Charles were fond of traveling. The desire to be non-communicative with the press was honored by Charles through the years. Deanna did participate in several interviews just before parting for France and a few during the intervening years.

Charles Henri David, born May 6, 1905, died on March 1, 1999 after forty-nine years of marriage. Fourteen years later, Deanna Durbin David died April 17, 2013 at the age of 91. Both Charles and Deanna were cremated, and their ashes scattered.

Deanna Durbin is perhaps best remembered for her singing voice – – a voice described variously as light, but full, sweet, unaffected and artless. With technical skill and vocal range, a legitimate lyric soprano whose tones were as clear as the words she sang. Her repertory included everything from popular standards to operatic arias.

The legacy of Deanna Durbin as a Hollywood star can be summed up from the notes from a showing of *First Love* by Toronto Film Society on March 2, 2015. "Deanna Durbin was one of the most amazing talents ever to blaze across Hollywood's sky. Discussions of great musicals/musical performers and comedies/comediennes always overlook Deanna Durbin. Yet her films received twenty-eight Academy Award (the first six films received ten nominations!) nominations in ten years (more than the usual people associated with musicals such as Fred Astaire, Ginger Rogers, Gene Kelly, Judy Garland, Barbra Streisand and Frank Sinatra). She received a special Academy Award in 1938 for her 'significant contribution in bringing to the screen the spirit and personification of youth,' and she garnered unanimously glowing tributes from a wide selection of critics of her era. She was an immediate sensation and one of the world's leading box-office draws from 1937 to 1942."

Over the course of thirteen years Deanna Durbin produced twenty-one movies, with nineteen of them box office successes! Her first film, without any prior movie credits except the movie short, *Every Sunday*, was a smashing success, both in publicity for Universal as well as money, earning a profit of $1,200,000, which translated today (2018), by the consumer index, at approximately $21,846,000.

Currently there are three internet sites for clubs: The Deanna Durbin Society, Deanna Durbin Devotees and Deanna Durbin Devotees Facebook.

> "What a shame that she never appreciated how much happiness she provided to moviegoers of all ages."
> - *Remembering Deanna Durbin*
> By Leonard Maltin
> May 2, 2013. (IndieWire website)

AFTERWORDS - medleys

Here is the section of the book where I can let my imagination run rampant and say what I want (within reason), without substantiation. For the period of time I was obsessed with Deanna Durbin these thoughts surprised my mind and found their way onto paper – or, more correctly, onto my laptop screen.

First off, after a bingeing marathon of Deanna Durbin's 21 movies, it struck me that she was a "commodity" – in a business sense – her voice and acting abilities paid a portion of salaries for hundreds – those working on the film: carpenters, writers, directors, producers, cameramen, etc. as well as photographers, promotors, theaters, right down to the persons in the concession selling popcorn. As the newspaper discusses Durbin's coming of age, the decision makers at Universal were considering the "first kiss" and the impact it would have on the fan base – the paying public and on the profit of the movie. Durbin, as a contract player, had very little voice in these matters. Her job was to sing and act! Of course, all those involved in decision making felt they were the reason for the success of her films. But when Durbin balked, they got a rude awakening as it became obvious who was the "reason" for the success of the film and the "commodity" wanted a voice in her career.

Even though the Durbin family lived but a short time in Winnipeg the city embraced her as their own as "their" Hollywood star continued to rise. She was dubbed by the local media as "Winnipeg's Sweetheart." There was extended family there and on occasion Deanna visited the city. It is reported after the movie *One Hundred Men and a Girl* she and members of the family visited Winnipeg and received a tremendous welcome. A website *Deanna Durbin: From Winnipeg to Hollywood (1922 - 1936)* by Christian Cassidy – a *Winnipeg Free Press* feature celebrated what would have been Durbin's 90th birthday with updated information, including her death notice. It is a valuable resource for information on Durbin's relationship with Winnipeg and contains many links of interest. http://westenddumplings.blogspot.com/2011/12/deanna.html

Frank Nugent remarked in his *New York Times* review (March 18, 1939): "To suggest that this 'teenish miss is glamorous, with a leer ringing the word, is not simply stupid but obscene; if we had any authority over the matter, we'd wash the culprit's mouth with soap and make him wait an hour for a rinse. Deanna is as glamorous as a field of daisies, or a morning breeze freshening the waters of the bay, or—or a tomato plucked at dawn, with the night-chilled dew upon it and the pungent scent of the vine to give it flavor. That—gentlemen of Universal—isn't glamour, but it's the quality that makes Miss Durbin the nicest person on the screen today."

The list of Deanna Durbin movie achievements listed in the prior chapters makes one wonder why there is no recognition by the Academy Awards, at least in the 50s or 60s, for her outstanding lifetime achievements. I personally see her retiring completely from movie making, shunning lucrative offerings, leaving Hollywood and never returning, as an insult to Hollywood!

The *Hollywood Reporter* "Deanna Durbin, 1930s Child Star, Dies at 91" (April 30, 2013) by Duane Byrge wrote: "At the time of her retirement at age 29, Durbin was the highest-paid female screen star in Hollywood and, accordingly, the highest-paid woman in the world. She reportedly earned more than $320,000 from Universal in 1946."

Deanna Durbin remarked in an interview with David Shipman in 1983: "I did not hate show business," she told him. Speaking in particular of her last four films, she added, "I was the highest-paid star with the poorest material — today I consider my salary as damages for having to cope with such complete lack of quality."

When I began my research in earnest, I turned first to *Current Biography* 1941 (H.W. Wilson revised 1971) with the thought I would find accurate information and reliable references. I was immediately faced with her birthdate year being incorrect: "1922." After reading through the article, I was surprised the references included *Collier's, Good Housekeeping, Ladies Home Journal, Photoplay*, etc. The first three I could accept with reservations, but *Photoplay*! So many fan movie magazines accepted the movie star fodder written by studio publicists whose only aim is to keep the "star's" name in print! I went next to *Fortune*, a magazine founded by Henry Luce in 1929, an oversize magazine (11"×14") with 100-plus pages and articles of "depth." On reading the October 1939 Deanna Durbin article, they too had the wrong birthdate year! I realized it would not be easy to locate substantial and accurate information! Interestingly enough *Life* (December 16, 1940) "promptly announced an error in their previous calculations: Deanna Durbin is not 18, but 19." I have concluded the problem of her age had to do with her birthday being near the end of the year and her PR department could plus or minus a year depending on the impact of age to the spiel.

The "Legend of Edna Mae" has always fascinated me in as there is no definitive narrative. Simply stated: talent agent, Robert Sherill, aware of M.G.M.'s need for a child singer stumbled across Deanna Durbin. He was impressed and took her to the studio for an audition. She was signed to a short-term contract and made a short film with Judy Garland. The interest in a child singer ended and Edna Mae's contract was not renewed with M.G.M. I have yet to find a date for Eddie Cantor's radio broadcast contract, nor for how many years the contract was for – I have read both two and three years – nor the date for Disney's *Snow White* audition, nor the date of changing Durbin's name from Edna Mae to Deanna. There are many names involved as instigators of Universal's interest. The training of Durbin fell to both Pasternak and Koster; however, Pasternak seems to be the primary teacher, yet I have read Koster son's Bob lamented to The Deanna Durbin Devotees his father did the most, using the argument he was director. In *Easy the Hard Way* (G.P. Putnam's Sons, New York 1956) by Joe Pasternak (as told to David Chandler) we read: "No one makes a star, of course; not the producer, not the director, not the writer. It is a matter of chemistry between the public and the player, and the player must come to the public, just as the public must come to the player to make her a star. Deanna's genius had to be unfolded; but it was hers alone, always was, and no one 'discovered' her or can take credit for her. You can't hide that kind of light under a bushel. You just can't even if you try." (p168)

Durbin, on several occasions, lamented the world of Hollywood stars and dropped many "hints" about quitting the Hollywood life. Researching her life and reading what was printed in fan magazines there is no wonder she felt as she did. A clipped photo from such a magazine shows Durbin with her parents celebrating Mrs. Durbin's birthday – the cutline read: "– which means that any difficulties between Deanna and her parents have been straightened out at last." Another clipping titled "Hedda Hopper's Inside Story of Deanna Durbin's Divorce," a rambling article, stated Durbin should have listen to Mrs. Durbin's advice and not married Vaughn Paul. Hopper goes on to say, "Deanna's divorce is not shattering news to me." Basically saying "I could have told you so!" And then there is the Joseph Cotten story of a tryst between Cotten and Durbin on the set of *Hers to Hold* at the studio, where, because of the late hour, spent the night in their respective dressing rooms. The next day they were seen eating together in the cafeteria – and the rumor mill went into overdrive! Cotten in his biography, *Vanity Will Get You Somewhere* (San Francisco: Mercury House, (1987), denied the encounter and it was rumored he literally kicked the chair out from under the gossip columnists who reported the "scandal!" The Bakersfield Californian (February 11, 1948 p28) column "Hollywood Roundup" by Erskine Johnson gossiped that "...Deanna Durbin's big new romance is Vincent Price, her leading man in *Up in Central Park*, who is also getting a divorce." It is assumed most "stars" pay little or no attention to this drivel and more likely view them as a means of keeping their name before the public. However, I can imagine it could finally get to you, seeing your private life exposed to the public with half-truths and innuendos.

In the book *The Powerful Rivalry of Hedda Hopper and Louella Parsons* by Amy Fine (April 1, 1997) you can read: "In an even more potentially dangerous move, Hedda tattled on Joseph Cotten for trysting with juvenile star Deanna Durbin while they were working together on *Hers to Hold* (1943). Cotten was never going to leave his wife," says Leonora Hornblow. "They were just having a little fun." Hedda's exposé was "extremely painful to Lenore Cotten, Joe's long-suffering wife," but her husband got revenge for both of them. "There was some huge event going on in the Beverly Wilshire ballroom. Joe saw Hedda across the room and came toward her, saying, 'I've got something for you.' He kicked right through the gold party chair she was sitting on, and its legs buckled. The next day Joe's house was full of flowers and telegrams from all the people who would have liked to kick Hedda in the backside but didn't have the courage. Joe pasted the telegrams on his bathroom wall."

In an interview, Dale Kuntz, known as "Wisconsin's Leading Film Historian," President of Milwaukee Film Classics, a teacher of film history at Cardinal Stritch University, a collaborator on a very successful book, *The Films of Jeanette MacDonald and Nelson Eddy*, plus a variety of activities with film series, TV host and radio commentary, remarked about Deanna Durbin: "Number one, it's said that she had the best voice Hollywood ever discovered. As much as I love Jeanette MacDonald, Deanna Durbin has a better voice." Dale in response to his writing a book about Durbin: "I have. I was working on a book, 'The Films of Deanna Durbin,' and she was not happy about that at all. I told her it would not be a biography, but the typical 'Films of' variety. I promised I would send her the manuscript before it was published. But I couldn't get it published! At that time, Citadel Press did not want to bother with her. They thought she wasn't that well known anymore, and it would not be a good seller. I went to University of Wisconsin Press – they wouldn't handle it. They all thought there was no market for Deanna Durbin. That's interesting because there is still a Deanna Durbin fan club in England." This interview excerpted from Sean Martinfield's article in the San Francisco *Sentinel*: "Deanna Durbin - The Femme Fatal of Noir City X-mas, Wed night at the Castro Theatre." (web site www.fabulousfilmsongs.com/deanna-durbin-femme-fatal/)

Deanna Durbin sang only four songs in her musical *Can't Help Singing*, but six in *Something in the Wind*, with its genre

listed as comedy! An integrated musical where songs help further the story or enhance a scene as evident with the *Kashmiri
Love Song* in *Hers to Hold*, led to speculation about the six songs
by Johnny Green and Leo Robin and their enhancement of the
movie, *Something in the Wind*. At the opening of the movie Mary
is posed beautifully in a radio studio singing *The Turntable Song*,
which reveals both her as a disc jockey and a romantic, dreaming
of love:

> "I love you!" how' – d'ja like to hear that all day long
> And not in a song, but in a sigh? – So would I!
> Well, that's the dream I'm dreamin' while the turntable goes
> 'Round an' 'round an' 'round an' 'round!"

The mood of this delightful tune, which will be reprised later
with Donald O'Connor and The Four Williams Brothers, will
be shattered by the events learned from Donald Read and Aunt
Mary Collins (Jean Adair). Read insinuating she was his grandfather's mistress and Aunt Mary revealing the truth, a heart-
breaking story which led to Read giving her a monthly check.
Read, failing to get a signed statement from Mary regarding the
matter plots with the family to get Mary to the house and settle
the issue – even if forcefully kidnapping her! Mary, on the other
hand, indignant at the attitude of John and the entire Read family,
fantasies a revenge. In the early stages of the kidnapping scheme
at the radio station, Mary's voice is heard over the loudspeaker
system singing, for potential sponsors, *Happy Go-Lucky and Free*
with the beautiful lyrics:

> "I'm happy go-lucky and free
> Like a gypsy in the spring
> Walking through the flowers I love
> Talking to the flowers I love
> Laughing at the showers I say
> What a day, what a beautiful day."

For a moment John is enthralled by the lovely voice as Charlie leaves to decoy Mary to the car. The "freeing" lyrics are nulli-
fied by the act of forcing Mary into the car to be sped away to
the Read's mansion. This song will be reprised near the end of the

movie with both Deanna Durbin and Donald O'Connor. Mary, knowing the truth about the checks, begins to enjoy the dilemma that the Read family thinks they are facing – a family scandal. She talks of settling for $5,000 for herself – then $995,000 for the baby! Grandma Read decides the issue must be settled and states firmly that Mary cannot leave until legal papers are signed. Clarissa (Helena Carter), John's fiancé arrives unexpectedly, sending the Reads into a further dither – all except Charlie, who has seen additional checks made out to a "Mary Collins" dated twenty years ago. He wants to talk with Mary privately about them, but Uncle Chester Read (Charles Winninger) will not give them a moment alone, which leads to Donald O'Connor singing the fantastic frantic acrobatic dance rendition of *I Love a Mystery*, revealing somewhat that Charlie knows the answer to the "mystery," as he concludes the song;

> It's so relaxing
> > You, you with that innocent face
> This time you are the women in the case.
> > Yes, you, you're getting away with murder, too.
> You're fooling my whole family,
> > But baby, you are not fooling me,
> Because I love a mystery
> > And oh, what I know about you!

Finally, alone, Charlie reveals his love for Clarissa; this and Mary's desire for revenge brings them together. Charlie tells Mary she needs clothing and also the place to shop for them. John and Mary go to the shop, suggested by Charlie, where a fashion show is in progress. John is embarrassed over the salesperson remarks about his "wife." He becomes even more rattled as he tries to explain. Clarissa, her father and Charlie arrive. The bandleader, performing for the fashion show, knows Mary and coaxes her to sing. Mary chooses the witty song *You Wanna Keep Your Baby Looking Right*:

> "You wanna keep your baby lookin' right
> > Don'tcha daddy?
> You wanna see her all dolled up tonight

Don'tcha daddy?
    I kinda think, I'd like a mink
        As long as you are able
    But if you're not, I'll tell you what
        I'll settle for a sable."

The lyrics, all in a similar vein, and Mary's antics toward John delights Charlie as Clarissa and her father, taken aback, leave in a huff, after Clarissa returns her engagement ring to John. At the house Charlie encourages John to woo Mary and a "spark" is lit – Charlie and The Four Williams Brothers sing *The Turntable Song* outside Mary's window after John arrives in her room. As they begin the opening of the title song *Something in the Wind*, Mary sings as the other singers depart. The lyrics reveal the moment:

"A funny little bird just sent word
    from the treetops
That you will be tops
    in my heart!
When do we start?

Kiss me and hold me,
    There's Something in the Wind
And it tells me
    we're gonna fall in love!"

John and Mary kiss. Grandma Read (Margaret Wycherly) views the scene from afar and later approaches Mary, spelling out how their "love" will "ruin" John as he will be disinherited. Mary reluctantly slips away and returns home, where she sings *It's Only Love*:

"It's only love and I lost out
    Is that a thing to cry about?
It's only love – you kiss – you part
    So I'll forget but will my heart?
One more dream warm and gay
    One more dream gone astray
It's only love, my love for you

And it will only last my whole life through
One more dream warm and gay
One more dream gone astray."

She turns her attention to her future and finding a sponsor for her radio show; however, Uncle Chester has other plans. He poses as John Read, over the phone, requesting that the police arrest Mary Collins for extortion. The police dragnet apprehends her at the airline departing gate as she prepares to fly to New York City for an audition. She is taken to the police station and placed in a holding cell where she meets Tony (Jan Peerce), a guard coming onto duty. He prepares to rehearse his part of an operatic duet, *Miserere* from *Il Trovatore* (Music by Giuseppe Verdi Libretto by Salvatore Cammarano). Mary offers to sing the female role if she can make a telephone call. Tony says, "No!" However, when Tony drops the cell keys, in retrieving them, he clips them to his belt, Mary agrees to aid his rehearsal with a plan to slip the keys off Tony's belt. Manrico, Tony's character, is awaiting execution. Leonora, Mary's character, pleas with the Count di Luna, who is in love with her, for her lover, Manrico – the Troubadour's release with the promise she will marry the Count. Thus, the duet between Manrcio and Leonora, *Miserere* (Lord, Thy mercy on this soul). Leonora tells her lovers that he is saved, begs him to flee. When he discovers she cannot go with him, he refuses to leave prison, thinking she has betrayed him, when in fact she has taken poison to remain true to him. Dying in her lover's arms she confesses that she prefers death than to marry another. Mary slips the keys from Tony's belt as he leaves to get the music score to prove a point to Mary's challenge of making a musical error; frees herself and calls John. A similar sadness is being lived out by Mary as she knows signing the papers, which gives her wealth, will seal her destiny without John forever. Meanwhile, Grandma Read, patching up the relationship between Clarissa and John, with a lie, announces that the wedding will go on as planned. Charlie and John retire together, drinking to their gloomy future, confess to each other their true love interest – John for Mary – Charles for Clarissa. The call from Mary is misunderstood in their drunken state, but finally John realizes it is Mary and she needs him to "bail" her out. John arrives and in a moment of tenderness they embrace, and he professes his love. Mary is evasive. John dashes off to make arrangements for her release. While John is making arrangements the attorneys, having tracked Mary to the cell, gets her signature on the legal document and give her a million-dollar check. Perhaps *Miserere* is far more tragic than the relationship between Mary and John, but her actions giving her wealth is a poor substitute for love – yet now John will not lose his inheritance.

All ends well and is consummated with song, the reprise of *Happy Go-Lucky and Free*.

When I first considered this project, I thought about how many people are intrigued about rating their likes and dislikes, so why not my fondness in regard to Deanna Durbin's films – maybe even offering my email address for you to send me your list! At the time it was easy to choose my least favorite, but in the classification of best-liked I was having issues in coming up with a definite "best." After watching all twenty-one films my dilemma was solved. I like them all! Yes, some are silly, but all of them are tightly scripted, well-directed with Durbin's acting superb! Yes, some of the movies could have had better co-stars; however, most did a fair job – some outstanding and others mediocre. In fact, watching them in order revealed a great deal about Durbin's maturity, both in her acting and her voice. Being a film *noir* aficionado, however, I am still drawn to *Christmas Holiday* as my favorite – hoping soon there will be a restored copy made available.

What's in a name? *Fortune* magazine (October 1939 cited often) noted Edna Mae's name change to "Deanna" "– her studio given name had to be made legal to prevent its improper exploitation." To make legal or to legalize, one must consider assumed names are often not considered the person's technically true name. In my research I have noted reference to Deanna Durbin wanting to change her name to – and here it becomes confusing. Many believe definitely that Edna Durbin's middle name is spelled M-A-Y and not Mae – so is the name change referring to the moniker May from Mae or from Deanna back to Edna Mae? The *Bernardino Sun* (October 14, 1943 p1) reported Durbin's divorce: "Miss Durbin, whose legal name is Edna Mae Durbin Paul –" which adds to the confusion. It was reported salary figures printed by Hollywood trade publication listed Deanna as "Edna Mae Durbin player." For years a photograph of a very young Deanna was being offered for sale at $400 because of the "real" signature, "Edna May Durbin."

Deanna Durbin had a military bomber named after her during the war, which was not unusual for glamorous Hollywood movie stars, but to have christened a Pullman coach named after her, well, that was different; however, as I was winding up my research, I found that in 1938 she had christened a 750 gallon Seagrave triple combination pumper (firetruck). The item was in the *Fire Engineering Magazine* (July 1, 1938). The new pumper was added to the Santa Monica, California Fire Department. The photograph attached to the article shows a pensive Deanna looking at the camera as she shakes hands with an unnamed gentleman. The firetruck was not named after her!

In Middlesboro, Kentucky's *Daily News* (June 4, 1940 p7), Frederick C. Othman – United Press Hollywood Correspondent wrote in his column, *With the Hollywood Reporter*: "Today we watched her (Deanna Durbin) make what movie makers inelegantly termed her first 'Pratt-fall.'" In the czardas dance scene in *Spring Parade* Gustav (Mischa Auer) challenges Ilonka (Durbin) to dance, bragging she could not keep up with him – finally whirling her around and around until – 'Pratt-fall.' The 'Pratt-fall' Othman mentions is today commonly referred to simply as a 'pratfall.' A slang expression which was first recorded 1935-1940. This is a practiced deliberate fall on the buttock. 'Prat' being a slang for buttock in the 1500s. The ability to fall and at the same time seem surprised demands training. Unfortunately, this film was not in color as Othman's description of Ilonka's costume: "a pair of red leather boots, knee high – a skirt and bodice of fine green velvet –" would have been very colorful. Seeing her with a babushka and Auer with leather pants and a large handlebar mustache convinces me the actual dance by Durbin and Auer was performed by trained dancers in similar outfits and a glued-on mustache. In *Three Smart Girls*, Deanna, following her opening song, responds to the call for lunch by diving into the water and swimming to shore. Running on the pathway to the house she slips and falls, quickly recovers and continues. It was not quite a pratfall, but well executed.

On many internet sites *Brahms' Lullaby* by Johannes Brahms is listed as being on the musical soundtrack of *I'll Be Yours*; however, in the movie, Deanna Durbin does not sing a lullaby. Perhaps the scene was a final cut, explaining the number of photographs circulating promoting the film, of Durbin with a young baby on a train that sped her away from Cobbleskill, NY to New York City. There is a town in New York by this name and is about 165 miles north of NYC.

Currently the only books known to deal exclusively with Deanna Durbin are: *Deanna Durbin: Fairy Tale* (May 1996) by W.E. Mills and the other, a manuscript, *The Deanna Durbin Story: A Revealing Biography* by Alexander McRobbie (date unknown). I have read that the Mills' book is a "long love letter" to Deanna Durbin. The other, by McRobbie, a manuscript which I acquired several years ago, can be summed up in the second section of the title, "A Revealing Biography." As of 2019 it seems that the Mills book is out-of-print and the McRobbie book is still looking for a publisher.

Sometimes it behooves a researcher to look in their own backyard for information! It was reported in the local newspaper, *Augusta Chronicle* (June 28, 1944 p1), that a capacity crowd of 1,700 persons bought $25.00 bonds ($18.75) for tickets to view the "southern premiere," at the Miller Theatre, of *Christmas Holiday*, starring Deanna Durbin. The event ticket sales plus donations above the value of the tickets raised $72,587 toward the Richmond County quota for the Fifth War Bond campaign. The Miller Theater, opened in February of 1940, was a beautiful Art Moderne-style building that featured Italian marble terrazzo, black walnut millwork and a performance stage framed by fluted columns and hand-painted art deco nude nymphs dancing panels. The Miller, recently renovated, costing nearly $25 million, is now the home of the Augusta Symphony orchestra.

Another *Augusta Chronicle* (August 6, 1941 p6) item was Walter Winchell's column *On Broadway* bylined by Deanna Durbin as quest columnist while Winchell was on vacation. It read like a PR-produced piece telling of the unusual gifts movie stars receive from their fans. Written in letter form opening with, "Everybody knows that your (meaning Winchell - author's note) tribute to someone you like is an orchid. And what a lovely tribute it is." The article goes on to name items sent to movie stars such as Shirley Temple, Henry Fonda, Veronica Lake, Ginger Rogers, to name a few. Closing her letter with, "I'll settle for just one of your orchids any time, Mr. Winchell." Several items were listed for Deanna; one such was a miniature music box from Charles Laughton and his wife Elsa, which had a drawer "where the original owner stored her beauty marks –"

A very interesting column in the *Augusta Chronicle* (September 27, 1937 p4) by Ed Sullivan, *Hollywood*, reported an interview Sullivan had with Deanna Durbin regarding her latest film, *One Hundred Men and a Girl*. "'From the time I was so high' Deanna told me over lunch, 'I could sing. I really don't deserve a tremendous amount of credit. God made me a singer and I just sang' – – Director Koster passed the table and she pointed to him. 'He deserves most of the credit. Those little things he puts into the picture, like the feather on my hat just showing over the top of the seats during Mr. Stokowski rehearsal. Then when Mr. Stokowski is calling the caretaker, Marshall, to take me out, Mr. Koster suggested that I call Marshall, too, not knowing I was calling the very man I was hiding from. Those touches are marvelous'." The interview reveals the innocence of Deanna as well as her naiveté to film making. But, does it? Perhaps it was Koster who was responsible for these novel ideas as the script story unfolds before or even during the takes or suggested on reading the script. Who knows? However, regardless of Deanna's exact meaning, a delightful cheerful persona is communicated.

Finding information concerning Deanna Durbin after 1948 on the internet is sparse, except for the elegies following her death in 2013. However, in our local newspaper, *Augusta Chronicle*, there are numerous references, some directly about her, others just mentioning her in passing.

A long, long article (datelined Hollywood – INS – International News Service) with the headline reading "Many child stars of the movies finding unhappiness at the end of golden years," by Hollywood columnist, Maralya Marsh, appeared in the July 23, 1950 (*Augusta Chronicle* p25) issue. The article lamented that many notable child actors under "the high pressure of Flickervilla – – tears down many movie moppets physically and emotionally." Citing Dr. Mason Rose, analytical psychologist – or Jungian psychology (ideas of Carl Jung) which emphasizes the importance of the individual psyche and the personal quest for wholeness – "Many of the famed child stars who traded in a normal child's life for swimming pools, shiny limousines and tinsels of film fame were only making a down payment on an unhappy life." Deanna Durbin "who is trying to make good a movie comeback. The transition between *Three Smart Girls* and *Three Smart Girls Grow Up* was too short in Deanna's case as her two marriages both ended in divorce." On October 29, 1949 (*Augusta Chronicle* p4) Walter Winchell, in his column refuted Mason's remarks with, "So you want to be a movie star? Deanna Durbin starred in a dozen consecutive hits. Then when she got unlucky to appear in two or three so-so's as Coast H'w reported. 'She's planning a comeback.'"

Walter Winchell, who appears to have been a champion of Deanna Durbin, remarked in his May 14, 1948 (*Augusta Chronicle* p6) column, "Reports that Vincent Price of H'wood is mad about Deanna Durbin are debunked by his steady with a lady medico . . ." Just after reading that I note in *Augusta Chronicle* (March 15, 1950 p4) Walter Winchell in his *Man About Town* column, "Deanna Durbin and Vincent Price have resumed . . ." Hum!

A Joe Pasternak item from the pages of the *Augusta Chronicle* (January 4, 1960 p22) revealed, "Pasternak, who zoomed to fame with the old Deanna Durbin movies – – 'says the fate of movies rests in a return to family entertainment.'" Pasternak, as producer, commented on the state of affairs with current movies as he announced his go ahead to film *Where the Boys Are*, which became one of the top grossing movies in 1960.

Having friends in high places, such as Mary Peppertree in the movie *For the Love of Mary*, pays off: The *Augusta Chronicle* (July 16, 1964 p25), dateline Washington – UP, article reported, "One time movie star Deanna Durbin and at least 220 other

Americans have had their U.S. citizenship restored since the Supreme Court's ruling (May 18, 1964) affecting naturalized citizens living abroad."

John Burlingame's United Feature article in the *Augusta Chronicle* (October 26, 1990 p20) reviewed *Over My Dead Body*, debuting with a two-hour premiere, as a light mystery made for TV series, with the opening based loosely on the 1945 Deanna Durbin movie *Lady on a Train*. Interestingly both female leads were named "Nikki."

As Deanna Durbin's clock ticked toward August 31, 1949, the date her contract with Universal-International expired, articles appeared with film possibilities. In *Variety* (July 30, 1947 p16) plans for a British movie were reported: "Deanna Durbin may make a picture for him (him being British tycoon J. Arthur Rank - author's note) in England." *Variety* (August 27, 1947 p22) quoted Miss (Mary) Pickford, "Deanna Durbin may play the role filled by Mary Martin on Broadway." They probably were talking about *Annie Get Your Gun* (1947). In *Variety* (January 5, 1949 p274) it was reported that "Mike (Frankovich) currently is in Italy, with plans to make two pictures there, and Universal is sending Deanna Durbin to Rome for an untitled musical in association with Salera Films, an Italian concern." In reminiscence of these notices from *Variety* a small article in the *Augusta Chronicle* (March 6, 1950 p10) declared under the banner, "Deanna Packs Bag for England" that she may "start her film comeback in England – – because the movie business is in her blood. A British company, she said, wants her for a picture - -"

Nearly a year before Universal allowed Deanna Durbin's contract to expire a two-line notice appeared in Variety (July 21, 1948 p54): "Deanna Durbin paid $85,000 for the Jimmy McHugh home."

Reading the list of possible film projects proposed during the sixteen-month hiatus of filming activity one wonders how Deanna Durbin was viewing her life. She bought a California home, valued today at nearly a million dollars, making one think Durbin was planning to stay active in Hollywood longer. I wonder – as she waited these months, participating in Universal-International plans that were never to be – if it was as if her future looked like the page that follow this page – *blank*! Her little hat feather slips through these words of mine – never revealing herself – now here, now there. Until finally, like the actor Dean Harens in the final scenes of *Christmas Holiday*, says – "You can let go, now . . . !" – and after August 31, 1949 Deanna Durbin departed Hollywood for a quiet life of obscurity, allowing her life – that "blank" page – to become a "perfect cipher, a blank page on which others write to suit their own purpose." (a quote by Kathleen Norris, *The Cloister Walk* p 223).

      Now, have I?

The End